HISTORIC ST. CROIX

St. Stephen • Calais

IMAGES *of our Past*

HISTORIC ST. CROIX

St. Stephen • Calais

RONALD REES

NIMBUS PUBLISHING

Nimbus Publishing Limited
PO Box 9166,
Halifax, NS B3K 5M8
(902) 455-4286

Design: Terri Strickland

Printed and bound in Canada

Front cover:
W.H. Edwards's photograph, taken from St. Stephen, is the oldest surviving panorama of border towns on the St. Croix River. It was taken before 1869, the year of the legendary Saxby Gale, which destroyed the spire and transept of Christ Church, St. Stephen, shown in the left background. The spire was never rebuilt. The following year much of downtown Calais and the adjacent waterfront suffered a devastating fire.

Title page:
Gates & Wentworth Mill, the largest lumber mill on the St. Croix, and, in the background, Ferry Point Bridge and the stores and warehouses of Water Street, St. Stephen.

National Library of Canada Cataloguing in Publication

Rees, Ronald, 1935-
Historic St. Croix: St. Stephen-Calais / Ronald Rees.
ISBN 1-55109-435-5

1. Saint Croix River Valley (Me. and N.B.)—History. I. Title.

FC2495.S3R44 2003 971.5'33 C2003-902600-0 F1044.S17R44 2003

Canada

The Canada Council for the Arts | Le Conseil des Arts du Canada

We acknowledge the financial support of the Government of Canada through the Book Publishing Industry Development Program (BPIDP) and the Canada Council for our publishing activities.

Acknowledgements

My thanks to Irene Rich, curator of the Charlotte County Museum, librarians E. Marilyn Sotirelis and Karen Herrick of the Calais Free Library, the St. Croix Historical Society, and the Charlotte County Archives.

Ronald Rees

Contents

Introduction

When delegates from Great Britain and the United States met in Paris in 1783 to negotiate the conditions of post-revolutionary peace, they eventually settled on the St. Croix River as the divide between eastern Maine and what is now southern New Brunswick. Although there was some dispute subsequently about the identity of the St. Croix, rivers in general make extremely convenient boundaries. No survey is required and, barring a major shift in the course of the stream, the lines of ownership are clear-cut. But however cleanly rivers define territory, the communities that develop in river valleys tend to merge or unite. Only when the river is a recognized boundary between nation states, or this world and the next, does the phrase "across the river" carry associations of division or separateness.

Until the Treaty of Paris, the inhabitants of the St. Croix valley crossed the river at will, camping or settling where they chose. The first inhabitants, the Passamaquoddy Indians, hunted in the forests, grew corn in cleared patches along the banks, collected clams and scallops in the tidal flats, and netted salmon and herring in the Salmon or the *Schoodic* (the Indian name for the St. Croix) falls. When Euro-Americans from farther down the Maine coast moved into the valley in the 1770s, they settled on both banks at or just below the falls, the head of navigation and a prime source of fish. Only after the Revolutionary War when the St. Croix was designated as an international boundary did settlers choose one side or the other, and even then decisions were not binding.

In 1783 about a thousand Loyalist refugees from Castine, Maine, settled at the mouth of the St. Croix River, where it empties into Passamaquoddy Bay, and built the town of St. Andrews. A year later, in May 1784, a further two hundred Loyalists from New York arrived. They had been unwilling to settle for the rough shores and sparse soil of Port Mouton, Nova Scotia, where they had first landed, and sailed up the St. Croix to the head of tide to settle on the British shore, where surveyors had laid out farm and village lots. The men and the two widows in the group each received a town lot along King Street and a one-hundred-acre-farm lot along the Old Ridge Road. They were also entitled to tools, building materials and, for three years, regular army rations. Joined by other migrants from New England and other parts of Nova Scotia, they formed a law-abiding if profane settlement. The Reverend Duncan McColl, in 1785, described it as "a mixed multitude of people from many parts of the world, without any form of religion." The settlement was named Morristown after Sir Charles Morris, the surveyor general for Nova Scotia, but the residents called it variously Schoodic Corner, Lincourt, Dover, and Salt Water. Only after the creation of the province of New Brunswick, in 1785, and the division of Charlotte County into seven parishes, was its name finally settled. The growing community simply took the name of the parish: St. Stephen.

With no Loyalist influx to swell its ranks, the settlement on the American bank grew more slowly. A survey in 1784 had designated it Township No. 5 but only in 1806 was it large enough or distinctive enough to warrant a name. Directly across the river was the section of St. Stephen known as Dover Hill and, in what seems to have been a light-hearted gesture, American settlers adopted the name Calais, the cross-channel neighbour to England's Dover. Downstream, Township No. 4 had been sold to Colonel Edward H. Robbins of Milton, Massachusetts (subsequently the lieutenant governor and speaker of the House of Representatives). It was aptly named Robbinston.

The chief natural resources of the St. Croix river valley were timber and fish. Each summer salmon, shad, and gaspereau moved upriver in such numbers that they could be taken with dip nets below Salmon Falls, two miles above what is now the site of the main international (Ferry Point) bridge. The valley was also heavily forested. Thoreau's "tall, arrowy" white pine, the source of naval masts and spars and general building material, was the most sought-after species, but spruce and cedar were also valued. Cutting was moderate at first and the operations small, but when in 1807 Napoleon persuaded Russia to cut off supplies of Baltic lumber to Britain, North America became Britain's only overseas source. In Britain, duties against imported lumber tumbled and prices soared. So reckless was the cutting to meet the demand that by the 1830s most of the large pine had gone, and the attack on the smaller pine and the spruce had begun. Both John Jackson of the *Calais Advertiser,* and the New Brunswick historian, Robert Cooney, warned that that the forest was a perishable resource and counseled restraint. But Cooney's cry of "lumber moderately, fish vigorously, and farm steadily" fell on ears deaf to any sound but the bite of an axe or the rasp of a saw. From his consulate in northern Italy, the Vermont diplomat and conservationist George Perkins Marsh issued his classic warning (*Man and Nature, 1864*) to North American and European woodsmen but it, too, went unheard on the St. Croix. The feverish cutting continued, reaching a second crescendo during the Crimean War (1853-56) when Great Britain once again found itself denied supplies of Baltic lumber. By the 1860s most of the accessible trees near the rivers were gone; to keep pace with demand larger outfits had to haul smaller logs over longer distances.

At first timber was marketed as round logs (for masts and spars) or as "ton" timber, logs roughly squared so that they could be fitted snugly into the holds of cargo vessels. But as cities grew and demand shifted from logs and ton timber to sawn lumber, sawmills multiplied. By 1820 there were more than forty along the river, in roughly equal numbers on each side. The largest concentrations were at Baring, Maine, nine miles above the head of tide, and at the falls and rapids immediately above St. Stephen and Calais where the river descends 72 feet within two miles. The falls were the lowest point on the river to which logs could be driven and the point at which dams could generate heads of water large enough to drive the saws. Mills clustered on each side of the lower river at the Union Dam about a mile above Ferry Point, at the Salmon Falls another mile beyond that, and at the Upper Dam just below the bridge at Milltown. Among them were the Brisk Mill, renowned for the speed and strength of its saws, the Speedwell and the Harmony, all named at a time when machines were objects of wonder and pride. By the middle of the century the mills at Baring and St. Stephen/Calais, were so closely packed that in some cases it was almost impossible to tell if they were in British or American territory.

To deliver sawn lumber from the mills to vessels waiting at the wharves below the Ferry Point Bridge, the falls and rapids had to be circumvented. Until the completion of the Baring-Calais steam railway in 1851 more than a hundred horses divided into six-horse teams hauled wagonloads of lumber along frequently muddy roads between Stillwater (Milltown) and Saltwater (Calais). After 1839, the horse teams could also use a railway track but the line was poorly managed and its operations had to be suspended after a few years. On the New Brunswick side the alternative to sending the lumber over the falls and rapids was to build board sluices around them. The first, built in 1792-1793, was a modest structure, a few hundred yards long and a few feet wide, but its replacement, built in 1803, was gargantuan: twenty feet wide and a mile and a half long. Sluices were also built on the American side but they proved less successful. The New Brunswick sluices delivered packages or "barges" of lumber that could be floated down to the wharves below the Ferry Point Bridge or, if necessary, to the Ledge, a deep-water anchorage a few miles further downstream.

The marketing of lumber was promiscuous and the border, to a large extent, was a chimera. To avoid New Brunswick export duty and a British law forbidding on-deck loads between September and May, shipments for Great Britain were made, or at least cleared, from the American side. There was no duty on logs, and New Brunswick logs could easily be floated to a Calais mill. Not even wars or official embargoes interrupted the traffic. In 1807-1808, when Thomas Jefferson banned trade between Great Britain and the United States, and between 1812-1814 when the two countries were at war, Maine lumber found its way to Britain and the West Indies in British vessels or, as they were called then, British "bottoms."

On arrival at Liverpool, Belfast, Boston or New York, the vessels as well as the cargoes were sometimes sold. The small St. Croix population could not regularly command return cargoes of British or American goods and manufactures so the practice developed of building ships along the river, filling them with lumber, and selling both products at the end of the voyage. New Brunswick vessels were usually sold in England, and vessels from Maine in the seaboard cities. Conditions for shipbuilding were ideal. Lumber was plentiful and cheap, wages were relatively low, and there was no shortage of shelving beaches on which to lay keels and frames. Yards extended downriver to St. Andrews on the British side and to Robbinston on the American. Several Calais and St. Stephen shipbuilders had yards on both sides of the river so that building a vessel was often an international activity. A case in point was the 1,762-ton *Break O'Day*, one of the largest ships ever built on the St. Croix. The Porter brothers of St. Stephen launched it at Calais in 1853. The master builder was William Hinds, a Charlotte County man who had worked in St. Andrews yards before moving to Calais. The *Break O'Day* cleared St. Stephen for Liverpool where it was sold along with more than a million feet of deals, 16,000 palings and 133,000 laths.

BIRD'S-EYE VIEW OF CALAIS, ST. STEPHEN AND THE TWO MILL TOWNS, 1879

In the 1830s and 1840s—the heyday of shipbuilding—wharves and shipyards lined both sides of the river for more than a mile below the international bridge at Ferry Point. Behind the wharves and the yards, warehouses, chandleries, sailmaking lofts, ropewalks, inns and saloons, among them Calais's notorious "blind tigers" (wild and disreputable saloons), jostled for position. West Indian rum was a staple on the waterfront and if not provided free as part of a work contract, it could be bought for pennies in the grog shops. Until prohibited by temperance sentiments, work at the yards and the wharves often began with a tumbler of rum and two of water, the dose being repeated at eleven o'clock and at four in the afternoon, and heralded with the cry of "Grog Ho." A "long sweetening" of molasses added to the rum produced a rich mixture known locally as blackstrap.

During the sailing season the waterfront bristled with masts and spars, and on outgoing tides the river blossomed with sail. The *Frontier Journal* reported 3 barques, 18 brigs, 45 schooners and one sloop at wharf at Calais and St. Stephen on June 13, 1849. Streets and saloons would have been crowded with sailors, many of them local men, who were more familiar with the ports of the Gulf, the Caribbean, Western Europe, and parts of the Pacific than with villages and towns a few miles inland. The travel may not always have been informed but, as Sarah Orne Jewett's Captain Littlepage remarks, it gave the seamen something more to think about than the election of the next town clerk. In the absence of a national press, local newspapers carried foreign news, especially when a war in Europe or a revolution in the West Indies or South America could affect local fortunes. The world also came to the St. Croix unmediated. Crews were international, even on locally owned vessels, and goods from abroad arrived unpackaged and uncontainered: fresh fruit, pork and hams from the West Indies, china from Britain, woolens from Germany, prints and wall hangings from Boston, beer by the hundred dozen from London, and wine by the pipe and the cask from France. For much of the nineteenth century, the tidewater communities on the St. Croix probably were the least parochial in their history. The Calais waterfront, one visitor remarked, was almost as lively and sophisticated as New York's. As Captain Littlepage laments, from a social point of view the decline of shipping on the northeastern seaboard was "a terrible loss."

By 1860, lumbering, shipping, and shipbuilding supported some 13,500 people at the head of tide. Below the falls were the border towns of Calais and St. Stephen and near the falls, two satellite industrial communities each named Milltown—until New Brunswick's Milltown made its independence from St. Stephen official in 1873. Although both Milltowns regarded themselves as separate communities, the main towns and their satellites shared municipal governments. An Ellsworth visitor to Calais reported two villages of nearly equal size, one at the head of navigation and tidewater and the other just above, with a combined population of about 6,000. St. Stephen and Milltown, New Brunswick, numbered about 7,500. All four communities were tightly bound. With four foot-bridges spanning the river, people moved back and forth with complete freedom, taking jobs, buying property, marrying, raising families, voting and holding office. Nationality scarcely mattered and it was not a requirement for holding municipal office. At least six of the Calais mayors were not native born. Many merchants, businessmen and manufacturers had establishments in both communities and, until restrictions on immigration were imposed during the Great Depression of the 1930s, they drew workers from both sides of the river. Currencies were interchangeable and until the 1880s bank notes issued by the St. Stephen Bank were distributed as legal tender by the Calais National Bank. The Fourth of July and Queen Victoria's birthday were celebrated with equal enthusiasm on both sides of the river and on one legendary Fourth of July celebration St. Stephen reportedly supplied the gunpowder. It seems that because Great Britain still feared invasion from the United States, the garrison at St. Stephen kept a well-stocked powder magazine. None of the powder was ever needed for the defence of the town and it fell from official notice until the appointment of a punctilious adjutant-general. On hearing of the magazine, he decided to investigate, and found it empty. Sharp questioning revealed that the powder had been loaned to Calais to celebrate the Fourth.

In spite of the success of their lumber and shipping industries, the tidewater towns and their satellites did not become, as the Reverend Isaac Knowlton had confidently predicted in 1875, the "Queen City of the East." Their prosperity depended on the timber of the St. Croix and the lumbermen had been profligate. In the eighteenth century, scaling and cutting a tree of more than a thousand board feet was common, but by the 1890s there were so few large trees left it had become remarkable. As the size of the logs diminished, the mills produced proportionately larger quantities of "short lumber"—shingles and laths for the building trade and bundles of shooks, staves, and hoops that could be made up into boxes and barrels. The final ignominy for the traditional lumberman came in 1904-1905 with the opening of a pulp mill at Woodland twelve miles above Calais, and the building of a dam that reduced to a near millpond the once wild and swift-flowing river.

Shipping and shipbuilding declined just as quickly as lumbering. Fewer boards, deals and construction lumber (long lumber) meant fewer cargoes, and in the shipping trade wood and sail proved to be no match for steam and steel. As elsewhere in the Maritimes, shipbuilders responded by trying to make better sailing vessels but iron or steel-built steamships were safer, more dependable, and they could carry larger cargoes. The building of wooden ships began to falter in the 1860s, and by the 1890s the industry had failed altogether. The last record of carpentry work on a vessel in Calais is dated 1910. By the Second World War, when the U.S. Government would have liked to build barges in Calais, there was not a ship's carpenter to be found. For a few years, newer industries filled the void left by the collapse of lumbering and shipbuilding. These new industries were developed with capital made from older ones, and most relied on imported raw materials that came initially as return cargoes in the lumber ships: South American hides for a tanning and leather industry,

West Indian sugar for a candy factory, and European potash and South American nitrates and phosphates for a fertilizer plant.

Buttressed by these and other new industries, the border towns managed to hold their existing residents, and even to attract new ones. Calais's population peaked in 1900 at 7,665. But it was a false dawn; ten years later it had fallen to just over 6,000 and today it is 4,500. St. Stephen and Milltown, which numbered about 5,500 in 1910, today have a combined population of about 5,000. The drift of manufacturing to the metropolitan centres left the tidewater towns, which had once been part of the commerce of the Atlantic, on the margins of their respective countries. The bustle and raw energy associated with lumbering, sawmilling, and shipbuilding are now memories, and a river that was once an artery carrying the life-blood of two communities is now an unused park-lined stretch of water, the divide between two countries that the framers of the post-Revolutionary peace had envisaged. There is only one wharf where once there were seventy and, more often than not, not one boat in the river. The main streets of the towns where shops, saloons, and hotels competed for space are now mainly thoroughfares. A measure of the reduced significance of the river was the renaming of St. Stephen's Water Street in 1971. That year, St. Stephen and Milltown were once again joined municipally and in the process Water Street became Milltown Boulevard.

Although the economies of St. Stephen and Calais are no longer fused, the communities remain close, and each summer they celebrate their neighbourliness by holding an international homecoming festival. The festival is also a reminder of a once truly vital inter-dependence. Few now cross the bridges to work, there is no linking street railway or bus service, and nationality is no longer ambiguous. Yet stores, restaurants, theatres, rinks, and public libraries continue to attract clients from both sides of the river, and the young still intermarry. The same newspaper and the same radio station serve both Calais and St. Stephen and an accident or fire in one community draws ambulances and fire engines from the other. And at customs, residents of the valley towns pass through with a minimum of formality. It is an official acknowledgement, valued by both communities, that after two centuries of shared experience a political divide has little ostensible weight.

Chapter 1

The River

MILLTOWN FERRY

The quiet waters above the falls and rapids, that could once be crossed by ferry, were known as Stillwater, the turbulent tidal waters below the falls were known as Saltwater.

View above Ferry Point Bridge at ebb tide

For vessels of medium to heavy draft, navigation ends abruptly about a hundred yards above the International, or Ferry Point, Bridge. Above the bridge a succession of rapids and low waterfalls descends seventy-two feet in a distance of approximately three miles.

St. Croix Island

Aerial photograph looking downstream toward the estuary of the St. Croix.

View from behind Robbinston, Maine

St. Croix or Dochet's Island was the site of the first European attempt at year-round settlement in North America, north of the Spanish settlements in Florida. Led by Pierre Dugua, Sieur de Mons, and Samuel de Champlain, a party of 79 French explorers and adventurers wintered on the island in 1604-1605. They named the river St. Croix after a cross formed by the waters upstream, and they named the island after the river. Immediately after their arrival, in June 1604, they planted gardens on both the island and the mainland. Fresh water had to be carried from streams on the mainland. Winter set in early—it was the period of the Little Ice Age when alpine glaciers grew and the Dutch canals froze—and the settlement was assailed by bitter valley winds and numbing cold that froze even their wine and cider. Demoralized, and ravaged by scurvy which almost halved their number, the survivors abandoned the settlement in August 1605 and moved to Port Royal, a sheltered site at the mouth of the Annapolis River in Nova Scotia.

Bayside view on the St. Andrews peninsula

GRAVES, ST. CROIX ISLAND

During the winter, thirty-five of the French party died and twenty more narrowly escaped death. Unable to store vegetables the men were quickly reduced to a diet of salted meat and, because the river was blocked with ice, melted snow. Scurvy ravaged the company. Excavations of more than twenty graves found that the teeth of the buried men had resorbed or shrunken roots, a telltale sign of scurvy. The only members of the party to escape unscathed were the dozen or so who did not sit indoors: "a jolly company of hunters," according to an account written a few years later, who preferred rabbit hunting to sitting around the fire talking about Paris and its good cooks.

Freshwater Stream

Before winter set in and pack ice choked the river, the French settlers drew water from this stream on what is now the New Brunswick shore. St. Croix island is just visible in the background.

View near the Ledge, St. Stephen

A long shelf of resistant black granite known as the Ledge, a few miles below St. Stephen, is a fixture in the toponymy of the St. Croix. Although it offered farmers only marginal pasture and hay land, large ocean-going vessels, unable or unwilling to "take the mud" at low tide in the shallower waters upstream, could load and unload their cargo in the deep waters long the ledge. During the first half of the nineteenth century, at the height of the lumber trade, the Ledge was also known for the number of its grog shops: fourteen at one count.

View near the Narrows

Except for a few sections along the lower river, and on the slopes of the ridges above St. Stephen, farming was of little consequence on the St. Croix. Above tidewater the land was littered with granite boulders and filled with alder and cedar swamps. Turnips, grown in riverside farms above St. Andrews and fertilized with a rich compost of mussel mud, rotten fish, rockweed and barnyard manure, were the only significant cash crop. Before refrigeration, when the only vegetables available were seasonal, the hardy and tasty turnip was a popular dish. It was shipped in boatloads to Boston from wharves along the St. Croix in a trade that gave rise to the old adage: "See Boston or die a fool."

View from Brandy Cove

A few miles above the mouth of the St. Croix, sheltered Brandy Cove was once ringed with shipbuilding yards. Among them was the yard of Briggs & Brewer, Robbinston-based shipbuilders who also had yards in Maine directly across the river. When oxen happened to be on the wrong side of the river when they were needed at either yard, then they were made to swim to the opposite shore. As the name suggests, Brandy Cove was also a place where from time to time brandy came ashore without benefit of customs inspection.

Chapter 2

Logging and the Lumber Trade

LOGGING CREW

Cutting began in the fall as soon as the sap had stopped running and continued throughout the winter. The tools were simple and age-old: broadaxes and crosscut saws for felling, smaller twin-bladed axes and Swede saws for limbing. A skilled axeman could swing both ways and he was paid extra for notching or chopping the trees before they were sawn. At the height of the lumber boom on the St. Croix, an estimated three thousand men and one thousand horses engaged in cutting and hauling timber.

The camp

Each fall, several hundred men from St. Stephen and Calais moved upriver to work in the woods. Logging was a winter occupation and the first requirement was to build a camp. The ideal site, or "berth," was near the centre of the area to be logged and within easy reach of a spring or stream. The camp walls were made from notched spruce or pine logs, laid tier upon tier, and the roof from long poles covered with birch bark or shingles. The roof could be of the gable type, rising from low walls four or five feet high, or a lean-to ("tin baker") resting on a seven-foot wall at the front of the building and pitching down to two or three feet at the back. Two "tin bakers" laid face to face made a double camp. The roof shingles, usually three to four feet long, were split from trees of straight and easy rift such as pine, spruce, and cedar, and kept in place by a heavy pole laid along each tier. A stone fireplace heated the early camps; a large hole in the roof served as the chimney. In addition to a camp for themselves, the lumbermen built a "hovel" for the oxen and draft horses and next to it an equally rough shed for storing hay and fodder. By spring the average campsite was a litter of firewood, kindling, whetstones, and empty barrels.

COOKHOUSE This cookhouse or canteen was of more sophisticated construction than the standard camp. Boards have been tacked onto a rough frame and the roof is of the salt box type rather than the primitive lean-to. The staples of camp life were baked beans, salt pork, codfish, black tea sweetened with molasses, and rum: "Hot bread and tea and pork and fish / And a steaming dunkie-funk," as one eloquent logger poet put it. After a day in the woods it was enough, he remarked, to "make your pulses thump."

Loggers

Loggers were a mixed bag of farmers, fishermen, mill and wharf workers, transient labourers and recent immigrants. As a winter occupation, logging could be combined with farming and fishing, and for young, single farmers it was a blessed release from solitary farm life and the monotony of ploughing and stone picking. Proponents of farming and rural life, however, regarded the woods as a dangerous diversion that threatened to draw young men permanently away from the farms.

In the camps conditions were primitive. The men slept in bunks or in "field beds" built up a few inches from the floor; boughs ("spruce feathers") or straw served as mattresses. In the field beds, several sleepers might share a single long blanket or quilt. Also shared were the bedbugs and lice that infested many of the camps. Clothing was washed only occasionally, underwear rarely, and for many there was no such thing as shaving or bathing.

HAULING THE LOGS

After the first snowfall, the work of hauling or "twitching" the cut logs or "sticks" out of the woods could begin. The twitching paths were narrow, just wide enough for a pair of oxen or horses.

Felled tree

By 1910, trees of such massive girth were rare and could be found only in the deep woods. For the benefit of the camera, the man on the right is holding two crosscut saws without too much interest from his partner.

Hauling the logs

Oxen and horses were the conventional draft animals but when neither of these were available reluctant cows might be pressed into service.

Yarding

Logs, cut into sixteen-foot lengths, were moved from the stump to temporary holding areas or "yards" where they could be loaded onto sleds or tumbled directly into a stream in preparation for the spring drive. Logs at some distance from a stream were piled in "brows" on slopes, or on ledges above a road from which they could more easily be loaded onto a sled and hauled to the nearest river. The log roads quickly became worn down making movement easier. Brows were made by "skidding" the logs along long level poles and then hauling them up an inclined plane with a rope attached to a "gin" pole at the front of the brow. For turning and rolling the logs, woodsmen used a "peavie," a large hinged hook attached to a stout handle.

LOADING AND SLEDDING THE LOGS

The sixteen-foot logs were moved from the yards to the rivers by horse-drawn sled. Once in the river, they mixed indiscriminately with logs cut by other outfits so each lumbering outfit devised its own distinctive mark either painted onto the butt-end of the log or imprinted with a stamping axe. Above the mills, the logs were herded into booms and then sorted and counted. Booms were simple structures of long, heavy logs joined at the ends by strong chains that were strung all or part way across the stream to restrain the floating timber. The boom master sold unmarked logs and the proceeds were devoted to maintaining the boom.

The drive

Now roll the black one over, now cant the white one back
Now try that bull right there boys, now boys please step back
Now try that bull right there boys, now shove it from the side
Now that's the tune we work to upon the St. Croix drive

— Billie Marshall

The last phase in the logging cycle was the "drive" to the mills. As meltwater from the winter snows filled the tributary streams, the logs were tumbled into the water and pushed and cajoled with pike poles until they reached the main stream. Speed and timing were critical as the main river had to be reached before the flood or freshet subsided. The logs had to be kept from jamming on rocks, lodging in shoals and getting snagged on the banks of the river. A large jam could block a stream from bank to bank and from the surface to the stream bed. In the slower-flowing main stream, progress inevitably was slow, the longer drives taking a week to ten days. At night the log drivers slept on the ground in tents and "dinnered out," i.e. they cooked over an open fire. Food, blankets, and tents were carried in large boats known as Wangan boats. After 1830 many of the drives were organized by river commissioners, and in 1847 the lumbermen of the St. Croix founded a log driving company (The St. Croix Log Driving Co.) to orchestrate the drives on the main river. The drivers were divided into three crews: American Rear, English Rear, and the Centre Crew. The English and American Rears rolled the logs from their respective banks into the middle of the stream and the Centre Crew kept them moving downstream.

THE DRIVE

LOG-DIVING SKIFFS

Log-driving skiffs were long, sharp "double-enders" that could ride easily in either direction over still or stationary logs. Armed with peavies and pike poles, the drivers performed delicate balancing acts to keep the logs free and moving. The pride of the river driver was his shin-high boots studded with sharp quarter-inch steel "calks" designed to anchor him to a floating log "like the claws of a cat." Even so, drownings were not uncommon as logs sometimes trapped drivers who fell into the water.

Pike poles The long pointed pike poles, which had a barb at the end, were multi-purpose tools used for freeing logs from backwaters and eddies, breaking log jams, and poling skiffs.

Rafting

Once collected in the booms and sorted according to their marks, the logs were taken to "rafting" grounds that had been laid out by the boom master. Logs, ton timber, and sawn lumber could be moved more easily downstream when assembled into rafts. The rafts were made up of a varying number of "joints" of 25 to 100 pieces—the number depending upon the size of the timber—held together by ropes and wedges driven into the logs. Below Salmon Falls rafting was essential, otherwise the loose timber would have been carried back upstream by the incoming tide. In early days, when there was a market for ton timber and masts, logs were loaded directly from the rafts into the hold through ports in the bow.

Sawmills and Dams on the St. Croix (opposite)

All the St. Croix mills were water driven. Dams constructed above falls and rapids built up a head of water that could be released at convenient times to the mills. The falling water turned a wheel connected to a crank that drove a saw or a set of saws. The earliest mills had a single saw but by 1840 sets or "gangs" of saws, which could cut an entire log into two or three inch boards at a single pass, were common. The rotary circular saw was introduced in the 1850s and although faster than the older saws it was also more dangerous, taking a heavy toll of fingers, hands, arms, and even legs. On the St. Croix the sawing season ran from early April through November. Hours at the mills were long; in 1860 workers at the St. Stephen mills struck for an eleven-and-a-half-hour day when they had been working fifteen. There was no follow-up report in the *Advertiser*, suggesting that the workers were unsuccessful.

SAWMILLS AND DAMS ON THE ST. CROIX

MURCHIE'S DAM, MILLTOWN, ON THE ST. CROIX

Sawmills and dam at the Union Bridge

The photograph at left, one of a stereoscopic pair, was taken c.1870 below the Union Bridge that is just visible above the falls in the background. The falls, about a mile above the Ferry Point Bridge, are crowded with mills. In the foreground is the Calais-Baring shore railway.

Mill and dam at Salmon Falls (opposite top)

At Salmon Falls the St. Croix plunges over a subterranean intrusion of resistant black granite exposed by the erosion of the river. It is the largest single fall on the lower river. Before the building of mills and dams, salmon, shad and gaspereau, which moved seasonally upstream, were taken in nets, and even scoops below the falls. The dams, however, killed the salmon run, and sawdust and other mill wastes devastated the general fish population. Both Maine and New Brunswick passed laws against dumping, but at the height of the lumber trade there was little possibility of enforcement. In 1872 a disgruntled fishwarden named Curran charged ten Milltown lumbermen with polluting the river. One admitted guilt and paid a fine of twenty dollars, but the others closed their mills, threw hundreds out of work, and threatened a complete work stoppage if the charges weren't withdrawn.

Granville Chase Lumber and Box Mills, Baring (opposite bottom)

Most of the mills were shells, a loose covering of boards over a frame solid enough to withstand the timber-shivering movements of the water wheel, the cranks, and the saws. The Granville Chase lumber and box mill at Baring occupied the same site as the mill–the first on the St. Croix—built for William Vance in the winter of 1805-1806. Vance fought on the Loyalist side in the Revolutionary War and lived on the New Brunswick side of the river until the mill was built.

At all the mills, the objective was to use as much of the log as possible. The round edges or "slabs" left after squaring the log made pickets for fencing or laths for building. The laths were tied into bundles of a hundred and shipped as deckloads to the seaboard cities. As the logs became smaller, these ancillary uses became more important. Even leftovers from the mills had their uses. Although regarded as a poor man's wood, mill wastes were especially useful for cooking fires in summer as they produced a quick, short-lived heat. But there was also much unsold waste. Sawdust, slabs, and edging pieces for which there was no demand were thrown into the river and once sodden sank to the bed of the stream or were washed up on beaches. Inevitably fish populations declined.

Mill and dam at Salmon Falls

Granville Chase Lumber and Box Mills, Baring

Float of the Granville Chase Box Company

At the box mills the logs were cut into "shooks" for making bushel boxes used at first in the handling and shipping of potatoes, beans, and fish. With the growth of the sugar and molasses trade, Cuba turned to Maine and New Brunswick for containers: boxes for sugar and hogsheads for molasses. Box shooks or boards, ready to be set up and nailed, were shipped to the sugar plantations. There was also a demand for lemon and orange box shooks in the Mediterranean ports and in the Canary, Azores, and Cape Verde Islands. In time the range of box products expanded to embrace, as the Granville Chase float demonstrates, ginger ale, chocolate liquor, and boneless herring.

GRANVILLE CHASE LUMBER YARD

The Granville Chase mill was the last of the old style export mills to operate on the St. Croix. In 1930 it was bought by the St. Croix Paper Company and the Eastern Pulpwood Company and continued to operate until destroyed by fire in 1933. It was never rebuilt. In the photograph, Maine's Governor Brewster is addressing a group of mill workers during a promotional tour of northeastern Maine in July 1925. His entourage, to the right, presumably had heard the speech before. At the border towns, Lieutenant Governor and Mrs. Todd entertained the governor and his party at the Todds' house in St. Stephen.

Gates Outside Mill

Saw mills were tinderboxes. Sawdust covered everything, much of it dry and some of it almost as explosive as gunpowder. Bearings were housed in boxes greased with mutton or beef tallow seasoned with small amounts of sawdust. Often the machinery ran so hot that the "gangman" or "shove-in man," who controlled the entry of the logs and the rate of sawing, would be shrouded in smoke and even flames. Lighting, when needed, came from whale oil lanterns and open-flamed "flares"—sheet-iron pots filled with wicking drawn through a vertical spout. The flares burned grease, oil and kerosene from which the gasoline had not been removed, as it is today. Once started, a mill fire was almost impossible to stop. The burning mill in the photograph was the Gates Outside Mill, so called because it was next to the main river. The fire started on an August afternoon in 1923 and, encouraged by a downriver breeze, had spread throughout the mill within minutes.

Chapter 3

Shipbuilding and the Waterfront

St. Croix shipyards

Along the tidal reaches of the St. Croix a sound more familiar than the thud of an axe or the rasp of a saw was the ring of a caulking hammer. "Everybody who had a place where a vessel could be built," noted one memoirist, "and who knew anything about building, opened a yard." Lumber and labour were abundant and comparatively cheap, and there was no scarcity of shelving beaches where keels could be laid and vessels launched.

ST. CROIX SHIPYARDS

The photograph is of a vessel "in frame." The general practice was to lay bed logs parallel to the beach and place on them the ways and blocks that supported the keel. Once the keel was laid, stem and stern posts were fitted and the vessel framed up between them.

CHARLES SHORT

Charles Short, the most celebrated of the St. Croix shipbuilders and designers, worked as a master carpenter at yards in Chamcook and St. Andrews before moving to St. Stephen. In the 1860s he and his brother John, also a talented designer, opened their own yards in St. Stephen and Calais, and downriver from St. Stephen at Oak Bay, Brandy Cove and Lower Bay, St. Andrews. Four other brothers, all trained shipwrights, worked with them. The St. Stephen firm was known as J&C Short and the Calais firm as the Short Brothers. When the St. Stephen and Calais yards closed, Charles Short spent five years building bridges and buildings for the CPR. He also built the lighthouse at Grand Harbour, Grand Manan. In the 1890s he returned to shipbuilding and remained active as a master builder until his death in 1898.

CASHMERE At 1,725 tons, the *Cashmere*, built by J&C Short of St. Stephen and launched in 1873, was one of the largest vessels to leave the St. Croix yards. The Shorts were comprehensive builders who carved their own figureheads, and made their own spars and sails. They also had an ironworks shop where they made all their own metal fixtures—from capstans, anchors, and chains to the pintle straps that attached the rudder to the stern. The photograph shows the planked hull of the *Cashmere*.

Rocklands (ABOVE AND OPPOSITE TOP)

The 1,506 ton *Rocklands*, launched on October 1, 1878, was the last ship built by the J&C Short Company. The launching of a large vessel was a gala event that could attract several thousand spectators. Streets, inns, and taverns were crowded with people and all the adjacent yards decorated with flags and bunting. Built for Zachariah Chipman of St. Stephen under the supervision of the Bureau of Veritus, the *Rocklands* received a 3.3.1.1. classification for nine years, one of the highest ever awarded by Lloyds. With a "hollow bow," designed to improve the lines as well as fend off heavy seas, it was also regarded as one of the handsomest vessels ever built on the St. Croix. Other attractive features were a magnificently carved stern piece and a finely moulded billet head adorned with elaborate scroll-work laid in gold leaf. The cabins were finished in walnut, satinwood, ash, and the finest local white pine. The masts, however, were made from Oregon pine shipped around Cape Horn; presumably, local pine of sufficient size was unavailable. But for all the care and attention that went into the construction, *Rocklands* was an unlucky ship. A few hundred miles off Saint Helena, on a voyage around the Cape of Good Hope, its rudder stock cracked. The repair, which involved closing the crack by wrapping a chain tightly round the rudder and then securing the repair with hardwood wedges, was done from a floating stage in a shark-filled sea. The *Rocklands* survived this mishap only to founder a few years later (1882) during a violent storm in the English Channel while en route for Canada with a load of steel rails. The ship's structure is thought to have been generally weakened by several rough passages around Cape Horn.

Rocklands

Schooner at wharf, Calais
(left)

Overloaded, undermanned
Trusting to a lee
Playing high-spy with the land,
Jockeying the sea;
That's the way the coaster goes
Through calm and hurricane
Everywhere the tide flows—
Everywhere the wind blows—
From Mexico to Maine

Schooners or fore-and-afters were the delivery boys of the northeast coast. Drawing little water, and averaging around a hundred tons, they could be found in every bay and inlet in the Gulf of Maine and the Bay of Fundy. Unlike the labour-intensive, square-rigged barques on which the crew had to climb aloft to set the sails, schooners could be worked from the deck with a relatively simple arrangement of ropes and pulleys. Most of the romance of sailing is associated with square-riggers. The exact origin of the schooner is obscure. A long, sleek vessel possibly named after the Dutch word for glide ("schoon"), it was first described by William Falconer in his *Marine Dictionary,* 1769: "generally a fast sailer, and principally employed in trade by those who made speculations where dispatch was requisite." A schooner could beat into the teeth of the wind and tack on a dime, allowing it to negotiate rivers and estuaries impassable to other vessels. This made it particularly well suited to the West Indies trade because it could search for cargo in almost any coastal creek or river. Although "sharp built," it could also take the soft mud and—in the St. Croix—"sawdust" in tidal estuaries. The schooner was the making of the St. Croix and the New England ports and, significantly, it was the last sailing vessel to remain in commercial use.

Vila Y Hermano

Built for a Cuban company in the Calais yard of Rideout and Lord, the 131-foot-long, 327-ton *Vila Y Hermano* carried a crew of six. A barque of equivalent size would have required a crew two or three times as large. Launch day in 1892 was a red letter one for the border towns. Attendance at the dock was by printed invitation only and dinner, on the deck of the *Hermano*, was a regular "dress" affair. For ten years the *Hermano* worked in the Gulf of Mexico, much of the time carrying southern pine from Galveston to Havana. She returned to Calais for re-coppering after the thin sheath of copper protecting her hull had begun to rot, exposing the planking to the ravages of the teredo worm. The *Hermano* sank and was lost in 1905 after colliding with a steamer when leaving Havana.

Calais dry dock

There were several ways of exposing the hull of a sailing vessel that needed repair. The least technical was to work the vessel broadside onto a sandy beach, remove the cargo and loose fittings, and tip or "careen" the vessel onto its side as the tide went down. The process was repeated to expose the opposite side. At the dry dock of Nickerson and Rideout, opposite Calais Avenue, vessels were floated in at high tide and either shored up or reefed in a cradle as the tide receded. At low

Calais Marine Railway

tide the dock gates were closed and sealed and the exposed hull could then be scraped, cleaned, or replanked. A third method was to haul the vessel out of the water by "marine railway," a device that consisted of a capstan turned by horses moving around a platform. At high tide, and by gearing down the capstan, the horses were able to pull a vessel up a rail track onto dry land and into a cradle.

McCullough & Tait's Brass and Iron Foundry

McCullough & Tait's Calais foundry supplied brass and iron work to the shipyards and sawmills of the St. Croix. It also did a thriving business in wood furnaces, ploughs, and general machinery that were shipped to all parts of Maine and the Maritimes. One of the founders of the company, C.A. McCullough, was born in Calais and for twelve years at the end of the nineteeenth century he was United States Consul in St. Stephen. Moses Tait, the other founder, came from Chatham, New Brunswick.

The Calais Waterfront

When St. Stephen and Calais were active ports, wharves and storage sheds lined the river and both towns crowded onto the shore. Except at the end of the sailing season, the river was a thicket of masts. The three photographs were taken on an early winter day, probably in the 1880s, and when lined up they form a composite image.

Hutchins sail loft and the Gates & Wentworth Mill

Sail lofts were long buildings with bare walls and clear floors on which sails could be hung or laid. Stoves, needed for winter heating, were hung on rods from the rafters. All vessels were supplied with two or more sets or "suits" of sails. Some yards made their own sails but most assigned the sail-making to independent sail lofts. In addition to sails, the Hutchins loft, like most of the other lofts, made tents, wagon covers, and awnings for plate-glass show windows.

Gates and Wentworth, the other enterprise highlighted, was for many years the largest lumber concern on the St. Croix. The Gates family, who came from Massachusetts early in the nineteenth century, were pioneers in the lumber trade. Giles Wentworth, on the other hand, was a schoolteacher who gave up pedagogy for lumbering after his marriage to Lucy Gates. He became the first Democratic mayor of Calais and was the first mayor to come from Milltown.

In the background is the covered Ferry Point Bridge and immediately below it the backs of stores and warehouses on Water Street, St. Stephen. When shipbuilding, shipping, and lumbering were in full swing, both towns literally tumbled into the water. On the St. Stephen side, where the current was swifter and the riverbank narrower, stores and warehouses were built on piers over the river. Today, the St. Stephen shore is a parking lot, and the Calais shore a riverside park.

James Murchie & Sons

Murchie & Sons was one of several lumber companies operating 'from the stump' to the finished product, which included laths and cedar shingles as well as boards, deals, and construction lumber. All the large lumber companies had offices, wharves and warehouses in Calais and/or St. Stephen. As a young man James Murchie, who was the son of immigrant Scots parents, acquired a farm outside St. Stephen and like most of his farmer-neighbours he spent the winters cutting and hauling logs. By the late 1840s he was one of the largest woods operators, owning timber licences on several thousand acres of crown land. He built a large sawmill at Milltown, Maine, in 1853 and at the same time built or acquired wharves in Calais to store his lumber, and vessels to transport it. By the 1880s five of James Murchie's eight sons, all of whom were natives of St. Stephen, were involved in a business that employed 250 men. James Murchie Sr. was also a key figure in the Frontier Steamboat Company of Calais, and from 1874-1878 he was a member of the New Brunswick legislature.

Murchie & Sons office building, Main Street, Calais (right)

Murchie workers and shore railway

Loading lumber at a Calais wharf

Before it could be shipped, lumber from the mills, and the pine deals (boards) in particular, had to be stacked and dried. On hot, still days the air in the tidewater towns, according to contemporary reports, was heavy with the smell of sawn lumber: the sweet scent of pine and the sharp, resinous aroma of spruce, reportedly *the* Calais odour. Spurs from the shoreline railway served all the Calais wharves. In the photograph, six coasting vessels are waiting at wharf to be loaded with lumber. Only smaller vessels capable of "taking the mud" at ebb tide could load at the town wharves.

Barques at the Ledge

Coasters and all vessels up to four hundred tons could beat up to Ferry Point with the tide, but larger ocean-going vessels carrying boards and pine deals to Europe docked at the Ledge, four miles below St. Stephen. Lumber for the Ledge came down from the falls in rafts or scows sculled by skillful oarsmen. Loading was an art, as the lumber had to be stacked in such a way that it used the full capacity of the hold and was in no danger of shifting during the voyage. The Ledge was also the place where larger vessels built at yards in Calais and St. Stephen were rigged and fitted out. To eliminate the risk of a vessel careening over at its launch, only the lower masts and lower shrouds were fitted and raised at the yard. If no local cargo was available when a vessel was completed it sailed to another port, usually Saint John, to collect one. Occasionally, for instance, Liverpool-bound vessels collected cargoes of Georgia cotton for the Manchester mills.

The Great Calais Fire, 1870

This remarkable photograph, one of a stereoscopic pair, shows the beginning of a fire that destroyed much of downtown Calais and a large section of its waterfront. Children playing behind the old post office, near the intersection of Main and North streets, on a Saturday afternoon in August 1870 reportedly set fire to a pile of excelsior on a shed floor after it had been removed from crates of crockery. The blaze spread quickly to nearby buildings and proved impossible to stop. It destroyed houses, a large part of the business district, and much of the adjacent waterfront. Eleven wharves and the thirteen vessels that were tied to them, three new vessels still on the stocks, the Nickerson and Rideout Marine Railway and Dry Dock, several shipyards and sail lofts, as well as warehouses and millions of feet of lumber were completely destroyed. It was a catastrophe made worse by man and nature. Several of the fire hoses had been improperly wrapped, causing needless delay, and because the fire occurred at ebb tide vessels tied to the wharves were unable to get away. As the tide rose, the vessels floated loose and, wrapped in flames, drifted eerily downstream. Also consumed by the fire were goods taken from the Main Street stores and piled on the wharves for safety.

RAILROAD AND WHARVES, CALAIS Calais had no direct rail connection with Bangor until 1899, the year of the completion of the Washington Co. Railroad that followed roughly the old shoreline route through Ellsworth, Machias, and other coastal towns. Trains ran daily to Bangor, relieving Calais of its dependence on the CPR. The photograph was taken from a point just below the Ferry Point Bridge. The tracks branching to the left in the foreground were a spur leading to the bridge. The large, four-masted schooner is tied to the wharf of the Washington Co. Railroad. The Railroad station is on the far right.

THE *COURTNEY C. HAUCK* AND SCHOONERS ANCHORED OFF ST. CROIX ISLAND

During the years just preceding the First World War, there was a renewed, but short-lived demand for wind-driven ships. Many three-, four-, and five-masted schooners were built in the Maine yards. After the war, schooners continued to bring South American nitrates and potash to a fertilizer plant in St. Stephen but in general windships could not compete with the faster, more regular, and safer steamships. The *Courtney C. Hauck*, 1,627 tons, built at Bath, Maine, in 1913, would have been towed in and out of the upper river by the tug *Henry Wellman*. The schooners were towed out on the ebb tide and released at the Ledge. The first five-masted schooner on the east coast was built in 1888.

The water-front, c.1900

By 1900, there was little traffic on the river. In both photographs the tide is at flood yet there are few vessels at the wharves. The three-masted schooner in the photograph is loading lumber, one of the last regular cargoes carried by schooners. But the days when the Calais wharves were piled high with lumber are long gone.

Empty and abandoned wharves

By 1910, the approximate date of this photograph, the waterfront was uncannily quiet. There are no vessels, and the wharves on the Calais shore have begun to crumble. In the immediate foreground are the CPR station and the railway, which is also showing signs of neglect.

The Cove, St. Stephen

Schooners were built in the cove immediately above Ferry Point Bridge and, for their maiden voyages, they were loaded with lumber. The first bridge at the Point, built in 1827, was a drawbridge that could be opened to allow the passage of vessels. Vessels built after the replacement of the draw had to be finished downstream. The hulls were floated under the bridge and the masts and spars fitted at the Ledge or at one of the downstream yards. By the date of the photograph, c.1910, the Cove, too, was empty and still.

Chapter 4

River Steamers

EXCURSIONISTS WAITING TO BOARD THE *CUMBERLAND*

In addition to their scheduled services, the steamer companies offered excursions downriver and into Passamaquoddy Bay. The outings, which were generally on a Sunday, became targets for vituperative clergy. The excursions that gave greatest offence were those aboard the sleek and luxuriously appointed *Olivette*, a "dark floating palace of hell" according to one Eastport minister, and a stage for "licentious goings-on," i.e. dancing and, most probably, drinking. The excursionists in the photograph are waiting to board the side-wheeler *Cumberland* at the Lower Wharf beside the former Steamboat Street in Calais.

Rose Standish

Until the 1930s, river steamers were part of the regular traffic of the St. Croix. In 1824 the steam brig *New York* brought two hundred people from Eastport to Calais, and two years later the *Eagle* began to make scheduled trips between Calais and Eastport. In coastal Maine and New Brunswick, where poor and often impassable roads forced virtually all traffic onto the water, vessels that could carry both passengers and freight, and run to a schedule, were prized. From Calais steamers ran to St. Andrews, Robbinston, and Eastport, where they connected with vessels for Portland, Boston, and Saint John.

The *Rose Standish* was built at Brooklyn in 1863 and served the Boston-Nantasket Beach Line until bought by the Frontier Steamboat Company of Calais in 1887. As a side-wheeler she was driven by cranks or "walking beams," visible above the upper deck, that converted the horizontal movement of the pistons into the circular movement of the wheel. The days of quiet sail were over. The revolving side-wheel, fitted with enormous paddles, made a noise that could be heard miles away. Like most of the steamers, the *Rose Standish* carried freight as well as passengers so it was not uncommon to see cargoes of hides, wool, and wood products piled on her decks. In the lower photograph, taken in 1898, the *Rose Standish* is at the Upper Wharf in Calais boarding men for Eastport, the first leg of a journey that would take them to a military camp in Augusta and, possibly, Cuba. All had volunteered for service in the Spanish-American War. The figures on the roof are a few of the thousands of well-wishers who gathered that day.

BURNT WRECK OF THE *ROSE STANDISH*

Although described as "fine, elegant and fast," the *Rose Standish* was no stranger to rough accident. During her first commission she was rammed and sunk in Boston Harbour but in waters shallow enough that she could be raised and reconditioned. But there was no recovery from her final accident. While being readied for the summer season, in June 1900, the *Rose Standish* caught fire at her mooring and burned to a shell.

GRAND MANAN FERRY

From the public landing at St. Stephen, steamers ran to St. Andrews, Deer Island, and Grand Manan. One dark June morning in 1912 the ferry collided with a dredge moored between the Narrows and the Ledge below St. Stephen. According to the captain and crew of the ferry, a hawser trailing downstream from the dredge swung under the ferry and became entangled with the propellor. The steamer swerved toward the dredge and the captain was unable to prevent a collision. The dredge, according to one observer, sank "like lumpy lead" and its captain was drowned. In the photograph, passengers are boarding the Grand Manan ferry on a wet spring day c.1935. The gun is a memento from the First World War.

THE *HENRY F. EATON*

Larger, more powerful, and less noisy propeller-driven vessels eventually replaced side-wheelers such as the *Cumberland* and the *Rose Standish*. The *Henry F. Eaton*, built at South Portland in 1901 for the Frontier Steamboat Company of Calais, reputedly was the strongest little steamer on the St. Croix. It was also the most accident-prone. On one occasion it crashed into a lumber pile, and on another it was beached on the Waweig River when the captain and crew, busy picnicking ashore with the excursionists, failed to notice the dropping tide. They returned to find the *Eaton* hard aground. Late one Saturday evening, when returning with a party from a dance at the Andrealeo Hall in St. Andrews, it grounded on a mud bank in the narrows. The passengers were put ashore in boats and had to walk to the terminus of the street railway at the Lower Wharf. The *Eaton's* heavy superstructure also rendered it vulnerable in turbulent waters. In the tides and whirlpools off Deer Island Point it would take such a heavy list that even the crew were alarmed. In August 1908, on its way from St. Andrews to Eastport, the *Eaton* crashed into a rock off Deer Island in dense fog. Holed, under full speed, and rapidly filling with water, it just managed to reach the American shore with the passengers huddled around the life rafts on the hurricane deck. When the *Eaton* was sold to the Eastern Steamship Co., the son of Henry Eaton, the Calais businessman after whom the vessel had been named, insisted the name be changed as he was tired of having his father's name "dragged through the sawdust of the St. Croix River." The *Henry F. Eaton* became the *St. Andrews*.

The steamer *New York* at Eastport

At Eastport, the St. Croix and the Saint John steamers linked up with larger vessels for the run to Portland and Boston. The largest of the coasting steamships were propeller-driven and had luxurious saloons, dining rooms and comfortable, if small, staterooms attended by uniformed teenage boys. In addition to passengers, the steamers also carried cargoes of canned sardines from the canneries at Eastport and Lubec, as well as general freight. The photograph of the *New York*, a sidewheeler, was taken in Eastport reportedly after the Saxby gale of 1869.

BREAKING ICE ON THE ST. CROIX RIVER

From late December until March the St. Croix freezes for about three miles below Ferry Point. To speed the spring breakup in times when navigation mattered, a steam tug would attack the ice, but if no tug was available, and the ice was not too thick, then a river steamer would serve. With the breakup, the *Courier* reported lyrically at the end of March 1884, "the whistle of tug and steamer, the roll of capstan and creaking of hawser, will now be our daily portion, while at night the dip of oar and the merry laugh of boating parties will tell that Romeo is still abroad. We are all glad to see the ice leave." Most pleased of all were the pragmatic lumber merchants of Calais who were anxious to clear their yards and wharves before the arrival, early in April, of the tax assessor. The photograph was one of a stereoscopic pair taken from St. Stephen in 1873.

STEAMER *JEANNETTE* AT THE LOWER WHARF

Because of the extreme twenty-foot tide, the St. Croix steamers had to have two wharves. At flood tide the steamers came to the Upper Wharf, just below the Ferry Point Bridge, but at the ebb they dropped their passengers at the Lower Wharf, Steamboat Street. As the tide came up, they made for the Upper Wharf to land freight. At slack tide, when the steamers could go to either wharf, coach drivers watched from Hinckley Hill to see which one would be chosen.

THE UPPER WHARF

Visit of Lord Willingdon

By July 1927, the date of Governor General Lord Willingdon's visit to St. Andrews and St. Stephen, traffic on the river had been reduced to pleasure craft and river steamers. The photograph shows the return of picnickers from McMaster Island on a foggy St. Croix day. The picnic had been organized by Florence Ayscough, a sinophile who donated a rich collection of Chinese artifacts to the Charlotte County Museum in St. Stephen.

Canada & Western Railroad & Boston Steamboat Office

In 1871, with the completion of the European and North American Railroad linking Bangor and Saint John, St. Stephen stole a march on Calais. The railroad connected with the St. Andrews and Quebec line—which in 1866 had been extended to St. Stephen—at McAdam Junction, and crossed the border at Vanceboro on the headwaters of the St. Croix about forty miles above Calais. Businessmen in Calais had lobbied hard to make Calais the crossing place, and after the lobbying failed they attempted to have the branch line to St. Stephen brought across the river. But officials of the two border towns could not come to an agreement on the building of a railroad bridge, a contretemps that caused ill-feeling for several years. Calais residents who wished to travel by rail could purchase tickets at an office at the corner of Union and Main streets. The town had no direct rail connection with Bangor until the completion of the Washington Co. Railroad in 1897. Behind the Canada & Western Office on Main Street are the mansard roof and portico of the St. Croix Exchange Hotel.

CANADIAN PACIFIC TICKET AGENT, LOWER NORTH STREET, CALAIS

With its own rail link to Bangor, Calais after 1897 was no longer dependent on Canadian railways for connections to the eastern seaboard and the interior. River steamers and steamship lines to Portland and Boston continued to operate until the late twenties and early thirties, but railroad competition was ultimately fatal to both. Freight rates by vessel were lower than those by rail, but railroad services were faster, less susceptible to weather, and available year-round.

THE *CAPTAIN LEWEY*

Built in 1853 by the Schoodic Lake Steamboat Corporation, a consortium of lumbermen and merchants from Calais and St. Stephen, the *Captain Lewey* was the first of the flat-bottomed lake steamers. Driven by a stern-wheel powered by two wood-fired engines, it drew only two feet of water. Although its engines and boilers, hauled upstream from Calais on the Baring-Princeton Railway, were engineered, the superstructure of the *Lewey* was clearly homemade. The covered midship section housed a dining area and two bunks for the crew. The *Lewey* towed rafts of logs, assembled from logs delivered by tributary streams, across Lewey's Lake to a point where they could be floated into the west branch of the St. Croix.

Chapter 5

Other Industry

Mixing Tubs

Copper tubs used for mixing ingredients at the Ganong Chocolate and Confectionery Factory, St. Stephen.

Fire at Red Beach Village, Wharf and Plaster Mill

A smoldering ruin, the result of a devastating fire in 1926, was all that remained of a mill driven by power from a stream flowing into a deep-water harbour. The mill had produced calcinated plaster for the building trades in the seaboard cities since 1840. At the mill, raw gypsum from the head of the Bay of Fundy was ground into fine powder, soaked in 220F water to release lime, dried, and then packed into paper-lined barrels at the mill cooperage. Lime burns when wet so it was important to keep the plaster as dry as possible. To meet the demand for plaster, the mill was supplied year-round by a fleet of five 150-200 ton vessels. In the 1880s the company diversified, manufacturing fertilizer from a mixture of ground bones, fish poudrette, mineral phosphate from South Carolina, and sulphuric acid. Like the plaster, the fertilizer was dried, packed, and shipped south in coastal schooners. A forerunner of the trade in manufactured fertilizer was the sale of raw gypsum, which is rich in lime, from quarries at the head of the Bay of Fundy to farms on the eastern seaboard. By the 1820s, farm fields had been continuously cultivated since the initial settlement and were impoverished. To avoid duties on foreign vessels at the American ports, the raw gypsum was shipped first to secluded inlets in Passamaquoddy Bay and then transferred to American carriers for the passage south.

Red Beach wharf and village

Until the 1926 fire, Red Beach was a considerable settlement. The fire, however, destroyed not only the plaster mill, but also the company store, a bridge, a wharf, and the post office. Neither the business nor the buildings were ever restored, and what was once an independent community became a suburb of Calais. Part of the old industrial site, which overlooks historic St. Croix Island, is now an observation and picnic area, landscaped and maintained by the U.S. Parks Service.

BIRD'S-EYE VIEW OF THE WHARVES, PLASTER MILL, AND VILLAGE, 1889

The calcining works and the plaster mill are at the head of the inlet. On the wharves are a cooper shop and a stave shed, a general store, and a shed for storing plaster.

Granite Quarry, Red Beach

The decline of shipbuilding and the lumber trade, accompanied in the 1870s by a general economic depression, threatened to impoverish Calais and St. Stephen. In a series of editorials, John Jackson of the *Calais Advertiser* urged businessmen to diversify their activities. Low wages and long hours, he remonstrated, had pushed labour to the utmost and it was now up to the capitalists to create new enterprises to staunch the flow of young people to the west. One new venture that would have pleased Jackson was the Maine Red Granite Company, a subsidiary of the Red Beach Plaster Company. Granite is not a scarce commodity but needs to be quarried near water for easier transporting because of its weight. In the 1870s, sources of red and black granite, then in demand for banks, mausoleums, public buildings, libraries, monuments, houses, and even paving and curbing stone, were found in the Calais area. Maine granite was exceptionally strong and able to withstand the pressures that developed—in the absence of steel framing—in the walls of large buildings. Ledges of outcropped granite formed along the St. Croix. It could be quarried easily withough stripping.

GRANITE MILL At Red Beach the granite was within a quarter mile of the ice-free wharf used by the plaster works, and near a lake-fed stream and a waterfall powerful enough to drive the machinery needed for cutting and polishing. The saws and lathes, manufactured by a Calais firm, were copied from machinery imported from Scotland by the Bay of Fundy Red Granite Company at Saint George, New Brunswick. Some of the Saint George workers were Scotsmen from Aberdeen, the "Granite City."

By the end of the nineteenth century, granite from the Calais area could be found in buildings and monuments throughout the United States. Red Beach itself was renowned for its long stones, used in the manufacture of columns and pillars. The columns of the court house in Kansas City, and the plinth that supports the bronze figure of Francis Scott Key, author of the "Star Spangled Banner," in the Mount Olive Cemetery, Frederick, Maryland, were both fashioned from Red Beach granite. The photograph shows a cutting and polishing shed. Stone, hauled from the quarries on large-wheeled, flat-bed wagons was sawn, cut and, if required, polished. As well as local stone, granite from distant quarries was shipped by schooner for cutting and polishing at Red Beach. Rough cutting was done on the beach, and the fine cutting and polishing in the sheds. Inside the sheds were large overhead cranes for moving the stone.

GRANITE-MOUNTED BRONZE PLAQUE

In 1935 there was a formal exchange of gifts, initiated by the Franco-American Society, between Calais, Maine, and Calais of the Pas de Calais, France. France sent examples of locally manufactured lace and several handfuls of earth from the oldest cemetery in the city. The earth was packed in a copper-lined, hand-carved mahogany box adorned with the French tricolor and the gold enamel seal of the city of Calais. In return, Calais, Maine, sent a leather album containing thirty-six views of the town and an inscribed bronze plaque mounted on a block of granite from St. Croix Island, the site of the first French settlement in North America.

The ritual cutting of the granite for the gift plaque by three Calais dignitaries.

GETTING THE GRANITE

Ganong Brothers chocolate factory

Fire at Ganong's

Ganong Brothers Chocolate Factory
(opposite)

James and Gilbert Ganong, co-founders of the renowned chocolate company, were born in Springfield at the head of Belleisle Bay on the Saint John River. James left for Boston in the 1860s where, according to family lore, he worked as a jockey. But weight was his nemesis and when no longer able to ride professionally he found work as a salesman with Thurston & Hall, a company that sold biscuits and crackers. Intent on starting a business of his own, and attracted by rising talk of a protected Canadian market, he moved to St. Stephen where he could continue to sell for Thurston & Hall and take advantage, once it had been implemented, of the protected market. In 1871, two years after his arrival, and with his brother Gilbert as a partner, he opened a high-end grocery store that sold, among other delicacies, Thurston & Hall biscuits. In a blue-collar community, the store barely paid its way, but candy did surprisingly well. By 1876 the Ganong Brothers were making candy of their own from molasses, sugar and coconut from the West Indies with which St. Stephen had long-established connections. St. Stephen also had good rail connections and, after 1879 and the implementation of Sir John A. McDonald's National Policy, the protection of a substantial tariff. By 1878 there were 150 on the company payroll, and by the First World War several hundred. Still thriving and in new premises, Ganong Brothers now has a payroll of more than two hundred and markets in the United Kingdom and the West Indies, as well as North America.

Fire at Ganong's
(opposite)

When lighting a gas jet in March 1903 a Ganong employee accidentally dropped a piece of burning paper into a box of flammable material. The fire spread rapidly, destroying much of the old building, including a second floor apartment occupied by Gilbert and Maria Ganong. An almost completed new wing was saved by a firewall.

St. Croix Soap Manufacturing Company

Two years after starting to make their own candy, the Ganong brothers, in partnership with James Picard of Calais, embarked on the manufacture of soap in a factory on Depot Street, St. Stephen. The caustic soda, greases and fats needed to produce the soap were all imported, the latter from slaughter houses in New Zealand and Australia. Before shipping, the greases and fats were packed in oak barrels coveted by the soap factory workers. Although the company manufactured a variety of laundry, bath and toilet soaps, it became identified with a single product: Surprise Soap. Rich in lye, Surprise Soap cleaned, so the advertising went, "the surprise way, without boiling or scalding." Produced in the form of no nonsense, ochre-coloured cakes or bricks, Surprise Soap could also be used for washing dishes, and scrubbing floors. Carpenters developed the habit of carrying a cake or two because they found that greasing spikes and screws made them sink into wood more easily. By the end of the century ten salesmen were permanently on the road marketing laundry soap throughout the Dominion, Newfoundland, and the West Indies. So successful was the company that in 1884 James and Gilbert decided to divide their growing empire: James concentrated on soap and Gilbert on chocolate. After the First World War the soap factory was sold to Lever Brothers and continued to operate until 1947.

SURPRISE SOAP WAGON

Surprise Soap might have been the answer to every launderer's dream, but it still needed advertising. In 1889 the company hired fence painters in Quebec to paint slogans on forty thousand square feet of billboards, fences, and barns. It also used a van, piled high with boxes of Surprise Soap, to take part in carnivals, parades, and summer band concerts. Another inducement, new to the Maritimes, was redeemable wrappers that could be saved and exchanged for gifts: a teapot, a baseball glove, or a lithograph for a parlour wall.

DOMINION FERTILIZER COMPANY

Located on the river just below St. Stephen, the Dominion Fertilizer Company converted nitrates from Brazil, potash from Europe, and phosphates from South America into fertilizer that was marketed throughout the Maritimes and in the Aroostook country of northeastern Maine. The factory was served by spur tracks of the CPR and by a specially built 225-foot wharf flanked by dredged berths deep enough to accommodate ocean going vessels. The raw materials were piled high in adjacent sheds and loosened with an auger. Despite closures and a major fire, the factory continued to operate until 1970 when it was forced to close because of distance from market areas and potato producers.

FERTILIZER SHED

Axe Factory, Dennis Stream, St. Stephen

The axe factory on Dennis Stream dates from the 1860s and the premises, despite many alterations and changes of ownership, produced axes and other edged tools until 1930. By 1913, when the factory was still water-powered, it employed more than forty men on two floors. Axes, chisels, hatchets, and hunters' axes were tempered first in charcoal and then, after 1912, in crude oil. Axes tempered in charcoal were guaranteed not to break.

Daly Brothers Shoe Factory, Calais

Like many New England and Maritime towns, Calais and St. Stephen had shoe factories. The larger of Calais's two factories was built in 1886, and although operated by a number of different companies over some fifty years, the enterprise was never more than marginal. To fund the first factory the town, a drive initiated by the Board of Trade raised $30,000 by subscription. But despite low wages, tax exemptions, and the availability of leather from St. Croix tanneries, distance from metropolitan markets in the end proved an insuperable obstacle. Importing raw materials and then exporting the finished product to distant markets simply was not profitable.

WORKERS AT THE CLARK BROTHERS SHOE FACTORY

St. Stephen's lone shoe factory (above) was on King Street. When the manufacture of shoes proved unprofitable, the building was used for food canning and then for the production of knitted goods by an American knitwear firm. The building was taken down in 1968.

St. Croix Cotton Manufacturing Company

By far the most ambitious industrial undertaking in the border towns was the building of a large cotton manufacturing plant. Between 1879 and 1880, a group of prominent local businessmen met to find ways and means of shoring up the ailing economies of the border towns, and stemming the outflow of young workers. Among them were James Ganong, and the former lumber and shipping barons. Textiles appealed because they had done well in New England towns and because tariff changes, introduced by the National Policy of 1879, gave a substantial home advantage to Canadian-made cottons. In Salmon Falls, the two Milltowns had ample water-power, as well as rail and sea links and, through the decline of lumbering and the closure of the mills, a pool of under-employed labour. But with no experience in cotton manufacturing to draw upon, the orga-

nizing committee was forced to look elsewhere for technical and managerial skills. Delegates from Calais and St. Stephen fanned southward and were able to interest an American cotton manufacturer, Lewis Dexter from Rhode Island, in the project. Dexter was attracted both by the prospect of producing for the protected Canadian market and by a $30,000 inducement bonus provided by the businessmen of St. Stephen and Calais. Dexter was also prepared to put up eighty percent of the capital costs, a windfall for the border towns , but the price of it meant the loss of local control of the enterprise. The cornerstone of the mill was laid with elaborate ceremony in June 1881, and in June 1883 the 34,000 spindles began to turn.

They were powered at first by water wheels and later by turbines driven by water plunging over the falls. Hydro-electric power from the same source also lit the two border towns. The cotton mill operated from 1882-1957 and, when all the spindles were in operation, it employed as many as a thousand workers. The photograph from below the dam (previous page, bottom) was taken during the spring flood of 1923 that swept away all the bridges except the steel bridge at Ferry Point.

Cloth hall at the St. Croix Mill

There were few jobs for women in the old lumber economy but at the cotton mill, where speed and dexterity counted for more than strength, two-thirds of the workers were women. At first, they took the unskilled jobs; managers, overseers, and second hands were brought in from New England. Most of the workers, too, lived on the American side, a preponderance that was reflected in the official holidays. These were Christmas, the Fourth of July, and American Thanksgiving. Dominion Day and Canadian Thanksgiving were workdays. A few New Brunswick papers objected to the American weighting but the Calais Times argued that this was reasonable given that the mill was built with mostly American capital, run by American managers, operated mostly by Americans, and manufactured American cotton into cloth with American machinery. Besides, the Canadian textile market couldn't support extra annual holidays!

MARCHING WORKERS, WATER STREET

The cotton mill was no stranger to workers' unrest. Within a few years of the implementation of the National Policy in 1879 the number of textile mills in Canada increased from seven to twenty. With the home market saturated, overproduction was a perennial problem and work stoppages, suspensions and layoffs endemic. Owning only twenty percent of the stock, the local community had no control over company affairs. In 1886 the entire workforce of seven hundred struck after a wage cut and, led by the Milltown band, the workers paraded through Calais. The strikers' demand was a modest one: a ten rather than eleven hour day. After the sale of the mill to a Montreal-owned conglomerate in 1892 even token community control was lost. All questions of production, pricing, and marketing were decided in Montreal and any resistance to company demands saw production shift to one of its other plants. In the photograph, six hundred mill workers are celebrating the return from Montreal of three union delegates who negotiated an end to a four-week-old strike. The workers met the delegates at the station and in drizzling rain followed their gaily bedecked car through St. Stephen and Milltown.

Wool-pulling factory, Calais

Wool-pulling was a spin-off from the tanning industry. The factory bought sheep and lamb skins, removed the wool, and sold the hides to local tanneries. The wool was shipped to Boston in large bales.

Chapter 6

Joint Festivals & Parades

Elders' Float, Calais, in the Diamond Jubilee Parade

Parades marking important civic or national events were international affairs celebrated on both sides of the border. For the sixtieth anniversary of Queen Victoria's reign, schools in Calais were given a half-holiday and the town was almost as heavily decorated as St. Stephen. Ministers and civic authorities from St. Stephen and Calais joined the parade, attended public receptions, and sat together on public platforms.

Elders' Float, King Street, St. Stephen

The Diamond Jubilee Parade assembled on King Street, St. Stephen, on the morning of Tuesday, June 22, 1897, and paraded through all four communities. There were six bands and dozens of floats that included a fifty-foot-long, manned warship, and floats from the Cotton Mill, Ganong's, and the St. Croix Soap Factory. The Elders' Float represents a kitchen and fireplace from the year 1837. Six men seated in one wagon were reported to have been ninety or more years old. The King Street photograph shows the formation of the parade in front of the fine colonial house of the antiquarian Arthur M. Hill, the planner and organizer of the float.

U.S. soldiers on Water Street

British soldiers marching down Union Street

Knights Templar in the Jubilee Parade

By the end of the nineteenth century, differences between Great Britain and the United States had been thoroughly erased. During the Jubilee celebrations, English soldiers marched down Main Street in Calais, and U.S soldiers and militiamen marched down Water Street in St. Stephen. Prominent Calais participants in the Diamond Jubilee parade were mounted Knights Templar and foot soldiers from Company K and No 6 Company of the 71st Battalion. These not only joined the parade but fired a royal salute and a "feu de joie." Other Maine participants were a band from Eastport, and fifty granite cutters from Red Beach dressed in neat white hats and aprons. All available steamers were chartered to bring excursionists and bands from Deer Island, Campobello, Eastport, and Lubec. The CPR also offered half fares from all its stations. The sidewalk, which looks newly laid, was made from water-tolerant hemlock boards.

GANONG BROTHERS

To prepare for the Jubilee parade businesses and householders bought some 15,000 yards of bunting as well as hundreds of flags. The house of St. Stephen's Mayor Whitlock is reported to have been "beautifully decorated" with flags and bunting, and portraits of Queen Victoria and several celebrated Englishmen. A large portrait of the queen in front of the Whitlock house was surrounded by incandescent lights; the letters V. R. were outlined in illuminated gas beside or above the portrait. The photograph above is of the Ganong Building on Water Street, decorated with flags, bunting and evergreen boughs. Covering the sidewalk in front of the building was a large evergreen archway, with flagpoles on each corner. Ganong's shared the prize for the best decorated public building with the Engine Hall.

Calais National Bank

Calais's oldest and best-known bank, at the corner of Main and North streets, decorated for a Fourth of July parade.

Company K,
"The Boys of '98"

At the outbreak of the Spanish-American War in 1898 there was a rush to the colours. The photographs show 73 officers and men of Company K, Calais, marching from the armory to the Upper Wharf to board the *Rose Standish*. They were en route to military camp at Augusta via Eastport and Portland. Although very few of the recruits got to Cuba, they were given a hero's send-off. Hundreds from St. Stephen crossed the Ferry Point Bridge to join their Calais neighbours in the streets, on the tops of lumber piles, and on the roofs of buildings, to wave an affectionate farewell. Mayor Swan addressed the crowd, calling for cheers for the company, which were 'tigered' again and again. The band played patriotic airs and accompanied the troops to Eastport along with a crowd of well-wishers. At the St. Andrews wharf, where the *Standish* heaved to, the company was cheered heartily. When an old Grand Army of the Republic (GAR) veteran reciprocated by proposing three cheers for England's queen, the response, both on board the boat and on the wharf, was, the *Calais Advertiser* reported, "one long to be remembered."

Grand Army of the Republic (opposite)

Every year they're marching slower
Every year the lilting music stirs the
hearts of older men.
Every year the flags above them
Seem to bend and bless and love them,
As if grieving for the future when they'll
never march again

When the Union soldiers came back from the war it was natural that they would have some kind of organization (the Grand Army of the Republic) to keep them together. On Decoration (now Memorial) Day, GAR veterans marched from Church Street along Main to the International Bridge, where flowers were thrown into the river in memory of lost sailors. From the bridge they then retraced their steps to Memorial Park, where a high school student read the Gettysburg address before marching on to the cemetery. Wreaths of fir, apple, and cherry blossom, made by ladies of the GAR, were laid on the graves.

Raising the flag

The photograph, taken on a fall or spring day about 1910, shows a flag-raising ceremony outside the Union Liberal (now Methodist) Church on Main Street. It was a period when ancient and modern forms of transportation overlapped: the pony and trap, the automobile and, just visible in the distance, a streetcar.

Grand Army of the Republic
(above and below)

Calais's One Hundredth Birthday Parade

If the Diamond Jubilee generated the largest ever parade on the New Brunswick shore, its counterpart in Maine was the parade to celebrate the centenary of Calais's incorporation as a town. On June 8, 1809, the Commonwealth, the Senate, and the House of Representatives of Massachusetts granted Calais powers to raise money, appropriate a burying place, build roads and do such other things as befitted an autonomous, incorporated community. For the 1909 centenary, invitations were issued to former residents and special trains were commissioned to bring these and other celebrants, from both sides of the border, to the town. The celebrations opened with an early morning salute of one hundred guns followed by the ringing of bells. For those who crowded into the Congregational Church, the reading of the original charter, poetry readings, and five addresses on the history and accomplishments of the town took up the entire morning. At the close of the last address there was, so the *Advertiser* reported, a "great rush" from the church, ostensibly to obtain favourable positions from which to view the grand parade. The latter was the "longest and grandest" ever witnessed Down East and the watching crowds, estimated at 2,500, the largest ever to gather in the border towns. The parade assembled on Washington Street and, led by the Calais City band and a platoon of mounted police, marched south along Washington to Main, then across the Ferry Point bridge to Marks Street, St. Stephen. After a circuit that brought it back along Water Street it headed for Memorial Park in Calais. One of the noteworthy events of the day was the dedication of a polished granite fountain given to the town by Henry B. Eaton, the lumber magnate. The granite was quarried locally and cut and polished by Red Beach workers.

SOLDIERS OF THE 55TH BATTALION

In May 1915, soldiers of the 55th Battalion assembled in St. Stephen before leaving for overseas service via a transit camp in Sussex, New Brunswick. Led by Shortt's Military Band, they are shown marching down Water Street on their return from church services in Milltown on May 8. Early the following morning, laden with lunchboxes provided by women from the churches and the overseas league, and boxes of cigars by well-wishers, they embarked from the CPR station. A chorus of bells and whistles at 6:00 A.M. had alerted the townspeople, some four thousand of whom gathered at the station. Among them was a large contingent from Calais.

ARMISTICE DAY PARADE (BELOW AND OPPOSITE)

The Armistice Day parade began at 2:30 on the afternoon of November 11, 1918. German capitulation had been expected for several days so plans for a parade were well in hand. The parade, a combination of bands, floats, returned men of the GWVA, Civil War veterans, Boy Scouts, and representatives from various organizations in both towns, was more than two miles long. It formed in St. Stephen then proceeded to Milltown where it crossed the Upper Bridge and then moved downriver to Calais. The bands played patriotic tunes, and soldiers frequently sang the popular First World War song "Over There." All through the day, celebrants crossed and re-crossed the bridges. In the evening, more than two thousand people assembled on Water Street in St. Stephen to listen to hymns sung by a massed choir from the churches of both towns and to speeches delivered from the balcony of the Queen Hotel. The photographs are of the parade; they show Red Cross cars moving down Water Street and bands, preceded by a mounted soldier, marching down Main Street.

Armistice Day parade

STATE LEGION CONVENTION, 1931
(ABOVE AND OPPOSITE)

Next to Calais's 1909 centenary celebrations, the Maine State Legion Convention of 1931 drew more people to the town than any other event. More than three thousand legionnaires registered and filled every available room in Calais, St. Stephen, and Milltown. The highlight of the convention was the Grand Parade made up of legionnaires from all parts of Maine, the band of the Pleasant Point Indian Reserve, and bands and drum corps from a dozen Maine towns. Other participants were the Saint John Pipe Band and the St. Croix Branch of the Canadian Legion. The parade gathered on Washington Street, moved down Lafayette to Main and then crossed the Ferry Point Bridge to Water Street. At the CPR station the parade circled and retraced its steps to the Soldiers Monument in Memorial Park. It was the first time that American legionnaires had marched in a body on Canadian soil and conducted services in the country. In the photographs American conventioneers are crossing the Ferry Point Bridge and the other members of the St. Croix Branch of the Canadian Legion are marching past the St. Croix Hotel on Main Street, Calais.

State Legion Convention, 1931
(above and below)

HURDY-GURDY MEN A hurdy-gurdy was a barrel organ or similar instrument played by turning a crank, and the hurdy-gurdy man was the precursor of today's busker. Like pipers and marching bands, hurdy-gurdy men were particularly appealing to children. Those in the photograph have been identified as Ganongs.

Chapter 7

Bridges and the Street Railway

THE UPPER BRIDGE, MILLTOWN

Built in 1824, the Upper Bridge was the first bridge to connect the two Milltowns. The first bridge across the St. Croix, however, was at Baring, built in 1820 to provide easy access to the sawmills (Upper Mills) on each side of the river. Like Caesar's bridge in the Fourth Book of the Commentaries, the Milltown bridge had a decided curve upstream so that during floods the onrushing water would force the constituent parts together. The photograph was taken in 1901, a flood year. Except at the spring freshets the waters above the Milltown bridge were still.

The Old Arch Bridge

The Old Arch Bridge was built in 1826 to serve workers in the mills and workshops at the Lower Dam in Milltown. On the Calais side, the bridge was elevated so that horse-drawn lumber wagons and trains of the St. Croix and Penobscot Railroad could pass beneath it. The St. Stephen end of the bridge was simply a long platform in front of the mills. When the supply of logs dwindled and the mills stopped sawing, the bridge was not kept in repair. By the 1920s the mills at the end of the bridge and on the New Brunswick shore had been taken down. Floodwaters have removed the platform and the old arch is clearly in need of repair. The photograph was taken from Knight's Corner, Calais, looking upstream.

FLOOD AT THE UNION, 1923

Built to provide access to the mills at the Union Dam, the Union Bridge was used chiefly by mill workers. It is shown here much the worse for wear after the flood of April 1901.

UNION BRIDGE

The record breaking freshet of 1923, following unusually heavy winter snows, swept away all the bridges except the steel bridge at Ferry Point.

Union Bridge, 1923

Covered Ferry Point Bridge

The first crossing of the river below the falls and rapids was by ferry. In 1827 the Calais landowner Colonel Joseph Whitney replaced the ferry with a drawbridge—the Ferry Point Bridge—to allow for the passage of vessels built in the cove immediately above. By 1844 the original bridge had worn out and its replacement was a solid covered bridge with no draw. Vessels built in the cove were floated under the bridge with their masts down. At first pedestrians used the same roadway as the horse teams, but later sheds for pedestrians were built on both sides. Teams travelling faster than a walk were threatened with a fine of $3.00. Like most of the St. Croix bridges, Ferry Point was a toll bridge.

NEW INTERNATIONAL BRIDGE

By 1890 the old wooden bridge was much the worse for wear. The supporting piers had begun to rot and the "life" had gone out of many of the horizontal timbers. The campaign for a new bridge coincided with a movement for the abolition of tolls. G.A. Murchie, Calais's dynamic mayor, spearheaded both campaigns and proposed that the border towns buy out the bridge companies. The campaign succeeded and on February 5, 1894, the tolls on all bridges were abolished. Schools were closed for the afternoon and at mid-day, as processions formed in Calais and St. Stephen, bells were rung, steam whistles blown, and cannon fired. The Calais procession crossed the Ferry Point Bridge and joined forces with the procession from St. Stephen at the CPR depot. After the confluence the processions moved through the two towns in a single stream. The new steel bridge, which was strong enough to carry a fifteen-ton steamroller, opened almost a year later, in January 1895. The construction was a joint enterprise, costs being divided evenly between the city of Calais and the province of New Brunswick.

Demon rum

In neighbouring port communities that had long regarded the free movement of goods and labour as a natural right, the tightening of customs regulations—spearheaded by zealous temperance societies and law-and-order leagues on both sides of the river—was resented. A long series of prohibition measures that began in Maine in 1851 and in New Brunswick in 1878 ended with national prohibition in the USA in 1920. But in border communities where it was possible, at low water, to carry five-gallon cans across the tops of the dams, and where customs officials in general had no stomach for the rigid enforcement of laws that defied established custom and practice, the movement of spirits continued. In the 1890s, when there was no legal rum available in Maine, and kerosene was expensive and scarce in New Brunswick, rum crossed the river in one direction and kerosene in the other. A versifier in the *Courier* in December 1891 celebrated the exchange:

Oh, roll me over a barrel of rum
And I'll roll you a barrel of oil;
We'll laugh in our sleeve as they take their leave,
And depart from their native soil

Let prohibition and customs laws
Essay our spirits to damp
We'll drink success to the good old cause
By the light of a kerosene lamp

Crowd scene, 1931 The purpose of a bridge is to facilitate and encourage exchange not to restrict it. The occasion in the photograph, although not identified, is most likely a dedication service held during the Maine State Legion Convention of 1931 when legionnaires from Maine and adjacent parts of New Brunswick converged on Calais and St. Stephen.

LESUER'S BUS

Before the advent of electric or motorized transport, ordinary people rode to work in horse carts. The carts were made as light as possible and the drivers had to stand in front in all weathers, reins in one hand and the brake handle in the other. The brake was to keep the cart from hitting the horse's heels. Lesuer's bus, a long barge drawn by two horses, was not, strictly speaking, a horse cart but it served the same function. It ran from Main Street, Calais, to Milltown. Canvas curtains provided some shelter from cold winds, and straw on the floor some warmth for cold feet. The photograph was taken at the junction of Main and North streets. Across the street was the third floor studio of D. Will McKay, one of the best-known of the early photographers, who opened his Calais studio in 1883. McKay apprenticed with W.H. Edwards of St. Stephen. In the late 1880s he moved to St. Andrews.

THE CALAIS STREET RAILWAY

The new bridge at Ferry Point, which opened in 1895, was the final link in a chain of steel that bound together Calais, St. Stephen, and the two Milltowns. In 1890 Charles W. Young, a prominent St. Stephen merchant and businessman, proposed the construction of an electric railway that would serve both communities. To satisfy New Brunswick law, which insisted upon a separate corporate entity on the Canadian side, a St. Stephen company was incorporated in 1891. Calais followed suit with the incorporation of the Calais Street Railway Company, in 1893. The former was then leased to the latter, which bought the rolling stock and equipment and hired personnel from both communities. The tracks ran from Main Street in Calais down to the Lower Wharf at Steamboat Street, and from Main Street to the Upper Bridge at Milltown. Once across the bridge the tracks followed the river through Milltown, New Brunswick, to downtown St. Stephen. The old covered bridge at Ferry Point, which had once supported Jumbo, a famous a circus elephant, was not considered strong enough to support an electric railway so direct routing from downtown to downtown had to await the building of a new steel bridge.

STREETCAR, NORTH AND MAIN, CALAIS

From the junction of North and Main, Bank Corner, the cars ran along North Street to Milltown, and along Main to the Lower Wharf in one direction and to the Ferry Point Bridge in the other. Passengers alighting from the river steamers at the Lower Wharf took a car to downtown Calais or to any point on the seven-mile route. At the Lower Wharf there was a picnic ground that became a very popular destination after the arrival of the "electrics." Women would pack a basket in the morning, take the children by streetcar to the wharf, and be home in time for supper. For shopping and entertainment, Saturday was by far the busiest night. The cars were packed and the main streets overflowed. The photograph was taken about 1890. On the left or east side of the street are two colonial-style wooden buildings that escaped the 1870 fire.

Water Street, St. Stephen

In St. Stephen the cars ran along Water Street and then turned up King Street for a short distance to Rose Corner. From Rose corner they ran along Prince William to the station of the Shore Line Railway (a branch of the New Brunswick Southern) just south of the business district. The last cars ran on All Saints' Eve, October 30, 1929, victims of the Depression, the cost of snow removal, and the door-to-door service afforded by the automobile. In small towns with relatively low population densities, fixed line systems were doomed once automobiles became affordable. But the closure of the line also suggests that movement between the two towns had slackened: fewer cross-border journeys to work, and fewer cross-border shopping trips. In August 1931, the St. Croix Motor Bus Company introduced a half-hour bus service that connected St. Stephen, Milltown, and Calais.

KING STREET, ST. STEPHEN

Chapter 8

Business Streets

LIVERY STABLE, CALAIS

All the large hotels had their own livery stables or were served by others in the town. The Fred Hartford stable was run in conjunction with the St. Croix Exchange and Border City Hotels on Main Street. With the change from horse to mechanical power, many of the livery stables became service stations. In the 1950s the site of the Fred Hartford stable was a Standard Oil service station.

Fire, Calais, 1940

When wooden buildings were heated by wood and coal stoves, and chimneys were unlined, few town centres escaped devastating fires. Two fires in the 1870s changed the complexions of both downtown Calais and St. Stephen. In Calais the fire destroyed a large part of the business district as well as many houses, lumber yards, wharves, and vessels. In St. Stephen, a fire of similar proportions levelled eighty buildings and thirteen wharves and left thirty families homeless. St. Stephen received help rebuilding from Calais. The charred ruins in the photograph were the result of a 1940 fire that destroyed the Cole Bridges garage on Main Street in downtown Calais. The fire spread so quickly that it almost claimed the lives of six mechanics, and burned so intensely that it shattered plate glass windows two hundred feet away.

KING STREET, ST. STEPHEN

The original name for what is now King Street, St. Stephen, was King's Mast Road. At the time of the Loyalist settlement, the Royal Navy could claim any white pine of sufficient length, straightness and girth to make a mast. Such trees were marked with the king's broad arrow. The most direct road from the source of the pines to the river lay along King Street. In the late 1860s, the probable date of the photograph, it was a street of finely proportioned colonial or Georgian buildings, many of which presented their narrow gable ends to the street. The street was unpaved and sidewalks were rudimentary. The photograph, one of a stereoscopic pair, is probably the oldest surviving photograph of King Street.

F. E. Rose's Grocery and Dry Goods Store, St. Stephen

F. E. Rose was a general dealer in corn, meal, hay, and provisions as well as groceries and dry goods (boots, shoes, and clothing). He conducted his business from a solid, beautifully proportioned Georgian building at the corner of King and Prince William streets, St. Stephen. In 1911 a fire that is thought to have started in a blacksmith's shop nearby destroyed the building and many of its neighbours on the eastern side of the street.

The replacement building, below, made from fire-resistant cement blocks, offered the same goods and services but from premises devoid of elegance or charm.

Courier Building, Water Street, St. Stephen

In 1864, David Main of St. Stephen bought the types and press of the recently failed, Calais-based *St. Croix Herald*. In October 1865, he began publishing the *St. Croix Courier* from a building on Water Street. As well as producing a weekly newspaper, Main ran a bookstore and operated a printing business. The elegant colonial building with its generous, moulded eaves and wide corner pilasters was destroyed in the devastating fire of 1877. The fire began in the hayloft of the Ganong barn and, fanned by a stiff breeze, quickly burned out of control, consuming much of the business district. David Main's business survived the fire but he was forced to move to new premises across the street. The *Courier*, with its sister publication the *Courier Weekend*, is still the newspaper of St. Croix.

E. C. Young Furniture Store, Main Street, Calais

E. C. Young's furniture store, established in the 1860s, sold furniture of every description, including pianos. Later, the range expanded to include carpets, linoleum, and parlour and kitchen stoves, so that a house could be furnished entirely from the Young store. At the time of the photograph, one of the upper floors housed the Olympia Theatre. After the 1870 fire, brick buildings replaced wooden ones on Main Street, and plate glass display windows the older small-paned windows.

Ira Leighton's Barber Shop, Calais

For centuries barbers were also primitive surgeons who bled their patients to restore balance to the bodily fluids that were believed to control human well-being. The red and white candy-striping of the barber's pole, which Ira Leighton has applied to his premises and his person, was an inoffensive substitute for the blood stained rag that was the first barbers' sign. Leighton's shop was on Church Street near the location of the current city hall. Beck's, next door, was most probably a blacksmith's shop.

Chase, Barker & Co., Union Street, Calais

The classically proportioned Chase, Barker hardware store stood on a site currently occupied by the Tourist Information Office. Like the buildings on either side, it backed onto the waterfront. To make optimum use of scarce waterfront space, waterfront lots were long and narrow. The interior photograph is of the office area at the back of the Chase, Barker store. A pot-bellied stove heats the store and, as in any well-stocked hardware store, goods hang from walls and ceiling and fill every available space.

G. K. Jones & Co., Union Street, Calais

The G.K. Jones building, near the junction of Union and Main streets, was one of the few buildings in that part of the downtown to escape the 1870 fire. As a plumbing and heating business, it sold parlour and office stoves, ranges, furnaces, steam and hot water heaters, tin and japanned ware, and all manner of plumbing supplies. The hay cart, one presumes, was top heavy.

Hill, Pike, Union Street, Calais

Winter and snow scenes are uncommon in early photographs. Cameras and tripods were heavy and took time to set up, and before 1875 the plates had to be hand-coated. The early plates, too, were not sensitive to shades of white so clouds, for example, were seldom recorded. Hill, Pike was a large grocery on Union Street, near the river and the wharves, that sold among other things molasses and West India goods.

North Street, Calais

In the second half of the nineteenth century the view down North Street (then North Milltown Street) toward Main would have featured masts, stacked lumber, and waterfront stores and warehouses. The sidewalks were made from rot-resistant hemlock planks and they were not entirely safe. Planks laid lengthwise were a hazard to mothers with baby carriages as the wheels slipped easily through the cracks, while planks laid sideways were traps for people with canes and crutches. In playful moods, children would try to step only on planks because it was "bad luck" to step on a crack.

C.R. Pike's Store, North Street, Calais

The C.R. Pike store, located on lower North Street just above Main, was a four-storied building that stocked West India goods (rum and molasses), groceries, flour, corn, pork, hay, lime, plastering hair, and cement. Earlier, as the faded sign on the second floor indicates, the business also sold seeds and farm equipment. Unable to compete with lumbering, shipbuilding, and sawmilling in the competition for labour, farming never flourished on the St. Croix. In theory, farming ought to have dovetailed nicely with lumbering, a winter occupation, but in practice farming suffered. Several commentators were critical of the amounts of basic foodstuffs that had to be imported.

Main Street, Calais, 1870s

The photograph was not annotated but it shows repairs to Main Street, possibly after the 1870 fire when there was some street widening and straightening.

MAIN STREET, CALAIS, C.1900

After the 1870 fire, brick replaced wood as a building material. New stores and offices were built with their eaves, rather than their gable ends, facing the street and with little regard for classical ideals of form and proportion. Historians in general regard the architecture of the last third of the nineteenth century, the late Victorian period, as one of the least prepossessing in the history of architecture. It did, however, allow for individual touches that would have been impossible under the restrained colonial or classical regime. The minaret on Kalish's Clothing House is an oriental flourish worthy of the Pavilion at Brighton, England. Bruno Kalish built it so his father might have some reminder of his homeland in the eastern Mediterranean. Bruno Kalish came to Calais when still a child. He was the second Democrat to be elected mayor, and the first Calais merchant to adopt the one-price system of merchandizing.

Main Street, Calais, 1940s

King Street, St. Stephen, c.1900

On King Street, which was spared a truly devastating fire, many colonial buildings survived well into the twentieth century. At the lower end of the street is a streetcar making its short run up to Rose Corner, latterly the terminus of the line. There are no automobiles and the street is still unpaved.

King Street, St. Stephen, 1938

The street railway has been removed and the road paved to accommodate increasing automobile traffic. But the sidewalk on the west side of the street is still wooden. The photograph was taken just above Rose corner, the junction of King and Prince William streets. The Rose building, with its awning and scalloped front, is about half-way down the street on the left-hand side.

Waterson's Drug Store, St. Stephen

Fred Waterson was a colourful druggist. He raced horses (pacers and trotters) hunted, and also served as the local "vet." Waterson's Great Heave Remedy and Waterson's A1 Scratch Cure were popular horse remedies. In his store window gifts and patent medicines had to compete for space and attention with stuffed caribou, deer, and ducks. It was a novel use for the new show, or plate glass, windows, and a reflection of the importance of hunting and fishing in the culture of the St. Croix. For many rural families, venison was an important supplement to the diet but by the end of the nineteenth century, hunting and fishing were recreational rather than subsistence pursuits. The hunting is still excellent, and several lakes around the headwaters of the St. Croix are well stocked with trout, bass, and land-locked salmon.

Bank of St. Stephen, Water Street

In 1886, the Bank of St. Stephen, one of the town's oldest banks, moved into the former premises of the Bank of British North America, a handsome freestone building with a mansard roof and an entranceway supported by Corinthian pillars and surmounted by a royal coat of arms. Like all bank buildings of the period, it was meant to express authority and inspire confidence. A 1908 trade directory intoned, with reference to the bank's directorate and capital reserves, that it had been founded on "the rock of solidity." Among the directors were Frank Todd, John D. Chipman, Henry F. Todd, and John G. Murchie, local men of "heavy" business interests and "long tried ability." Yet on "Black Monday," March 7, 1910, the bank closed its doors. The failure of a locally owned bank directed by the town's most prominent businessmen sent a tremor through the community and through the banking system. Stockholders and depositors lost heavily. An official inquiry by the Bank of New Brunswick pointed to the cumulative effect of poor investments and ill-advised loans. The premises reverted to the Bank of BNA which, in 1918, merged with the Bank of Montreal. In the photograph, the building behind the bank is the Ganong Brothers factory.

Bank of Nova Scotia, Water Street

Banks made from wood rather than stone could acquire an air of permanence and authority through the adoption of a classical facade. The St. Stephen branch of the Bank of Nova Scotia, with its temple-like facade, opened in 1882. In 1910 the bank moved into new premises on Water Street and the new owner of the building, J. R. Sederquest, a funeral director, raised the main building and the pediment to create two storeys. He also removed the two interior columns to make room for a large plate-glass window. Sederquest had large greenhouses on the edge of town in which he grew potted plants and cut flowers for funerals, weddings and social functions.

Fire on Water Street, St. Stephen

In January 1930 fire destroyed eight buildings and thirteen stores in "Dry Goods Row" on Water Street just below the Ferry Point bridge. The fire, which started at the back of one of the buildings, swept around a firewall to engulf neighbouring buildings. Another firewall downwind from the first, however, prevented the fire from destroying the entire street. The backs of the properties on Dry Goods Row overhung the river but the fire, ironically, could not be attacked from the rear. A rising tide prevented the firemen from standing behind the buildings and an attempt to bring a Coast Guard cutter upriver from the public landing through ice-covered water failed. Firemen fought the blaze for seven hours. In the photograph, firemen are hosing down buildings at 9:00 on a Sunday morning, four hours after the discovery of the fire.

Fire on Water St. (above and below)

Chapter 9

Grand Houses, Hotels, & Public Buildings

AMERICAN HOUSE, CALAIS AVENUE

At the time of its construction in the 1840s, Calais's American House was the only brick hotel east of Bangor. Within half a block of Main Street and a busy waterfront, it was one of the town's leading hotels. It was first named Calais House, but in 1876 a new owner, Dan Gardner, changed the name to American House. The owner at the time of the photograph, John G. Hamilton, a native of Yarmouth, Nova Scotia, had a reputation as a great hunter and bear slayer. American House offered every convenience: steam heat, electric bells, sample rooms for travelling salesmen, and a first class livery stable. The hotel's coaches attended all trains and boats.

Masonic Hall, Calais Avenue

Since 1911, when the American House closed its doors, the building has been a Masonic hall. A porch was added, and on the lower floors, large-paned windows replaced the small-paned colonial ones.

Calais Avenue

Divided by a tree-lined median and flanked by fine houses, Calais Avenue (formerly Church Avenue) was the town's show street and only one of two avenues in Maine to be designated significant by both the State Park and the National Park Service. The figure in the foreground of the photograph on the left, who has attracted the attention of the mounted girl and her attendants, appears to be a hobo, one of the many who ranged through the country after the Civil War. The girl, as was then the custom, is riding side-saddle. The American House is on the left.

WINDSOR HOTEL, ST. STEPHEN

Until the age of the automobile, most urban hotels were downtown, convenient to railway stations and, in port towns, to passenger wharves. The fifty-room Windsor Hotel, at the corner of Marks and Water streets, was built in 1891 by a consortium of prominent local businessmen who then leased the building. The Windsor was for many years St. Stephen's finest hotel. On the main street, and close to wholesale and retail houses as well the station and the steamboat wharf, it was convenient for both tourists and commercial travellers. Like all leading hotels, it had its own livery stable and Windsor coaches met every train and steamboat. A mark of the Windsor's refinement, and one that featured prominently in its advertising, was a separate Ladies' Parlour. Next to the hotel is the Bank of Nova Scotia with its classical, temple-like facade.

Queen Hotel, St. Stephen

The Windsor's St. Stephen rival, the Queen Hotel, occupied the lot on Water Street granted to Captain Nehemiah Marks, the leader of the Loyalist contingent who founded St. Stephen. Until converted into a hotel in the 1880s, the property remained in the hands of the Marks family. The Queen long survived its more prestigious neighbour, the Windsor. In 1915 the owner of the Queen bought the Windsor at a public auction and used it as an annex. Guests at the Windsor dined at the Queen. The hotel remained popular until the middle of the last century. In the photograph the building next to the Queen was the then new Bank of Nova Scotia, built in 1910 and evidently fire-resistant: fire has destroyed the roof of the adjoining building but the bank is undamaged.

BORDER CITY HOTEL, CALAIS

Two of Calais's busiest commercial hotels were the Border City Hotel and its neighbour the St. Croix Hotel, both on Main Street. In a continent affected by temperance sentiments, Calais and St. Stephen hotels were popular with travelling salesmen. Liquor was always available along the border, and at weekends the hotels tended to fill up. During U.S. national prohibition in the 1920s, liquor in Calais was only a bridge or a bootlegger away. The Border City Hotel had several incarnations, ending its days as the Emmans Hotel.

ANDREWS HOTEL

One of the few dry hotels in the border towns was, ironically, the one nearest the Ferry Point Bridge. In 1892 at the age of sixty-eight, Israel Andrews moved into Calais from Grand Lake Stream and opened the River View House (later renamed the Andrews Hotel) on Main Street near the bridge. At Grand Lake Andrews had been the blacksmith at Shaw's tannery and a renowned hunter and sharpshooter. His wife described him as a strong temperance man who would not have any liquor around. For Israel Andrews the regimen worked. Into his late eighties he could thread a needle, read without glasses, walk the length and breadth of Calais, and do all the buying for the hotel.

MANSION HOUSE, ROBBINSTON

Mansion House, on the shore of the St. Croix about twelve miles below Calais, was the home of General John Brewer, a shipbuilder, a brigadier general in the Washington County Militia, and a son-in-law of Nehemiah Marks, the Loyalist founder of St. Stephen. He built the Mansion House in 1785, a two-storey, wooden clapboard building with the construction date engraved above the fanlight over the front door. A glass-enclosed cupola above the roof of the house commands a fine view of the river and the bay and, according to Robbinston lore, it was a lookout post for spotters of British ships during the war of 1812. From 1864 until 1882, the house was the summer home of James Shepherd Pike, a renowned journalist, politician, and, during the Civil War, a United States minister to the Netherlands. Many dignitaries visited Pike's house in Robbinston, among them Horace Greeley and Charles Dana of the New York *Tribune*, and Salmon P. Chase, Senator, Secretary of the Treasury and Chief Justice of the Supreme Court. Pike was a horse fancier, and to time his pacers he put up granite milestones—which still stand—between his house and Calais. Pike also added the Greek-Revival porch to the front of the house.

Brewer House, Robbinston

Captain John Nehemiah Marks Brewer, the son of General John Brewer, was also a shipbuilder and an officer in the militia. During the War of 1812 he was a captain of militia. In partnership with Joshua Briggs, he is reported to have launched more than a hundred vessels from their yards in Robbinston and St. Andrews. Between 1828 and 1830 he built, across from the Robbinston shipyard, an elegant Greek Revival, amphiprostyle house: a house with columns on front and back but not on the sides. Other distinctive features of the house are French nine-over-nine windows with carved Grecian mouldings, Ionic pilasters with heavy entablatures, marble fireplaces, heavy panelled doors, silver doorknobs, and elliptical staircases. Like its neighbour, the Mansion House of General John Brewer, Brewer House is on the National Register of Historic Places. Today it is an elegant inn and antique shop.

Henrietta Brewer House

Some thirty years after her husband John N. M. Brewer had built the classical, temple-like Brewer House, Henrietta Brewer built a house of a completely different design. Frustrated by classical restraints, in the second half of the nineteenth century architects experimented with freer forms that allowed more latitude in the arrangement of rooms and the design of exteriors. In what became known as the neo-Gothic style, accents shifted to the vertical, shapes became more irregular and buildings acquired decorative detail. With its steeply pitched roofs, pinnacles, pointed arch windows and clustered gables, the Henrietta Brewer House, built between 1861 and 1863, has been described as the most authentically neo-Gothic house in eastern Maine. Beautifully situated on the banks of the St. Croix, the Henrietta Brewer House, like its classical neighbour, is also a tourist home.

Lonicera Hall, Union Street, St. Stephen

From a socio-economic point of view, Lonicera Hall may be the most significant house in St. Stephen. Built in 1841 for the shipbuilder James Porter, the original house faced the river. As in many port towns, the streets were mere paths that gave access to the houses and the main highway: the sea or the river. On Union Street many of the original houses looked onto the river, turning their backs to the street. But by 1903, the year in which Gilbert and Maria Ganong bought the Porter house, there was very little traffic on the river and on the inland side of Water Street bulky commercial buildings had replaced the remaining houses. To spare themselves daily views of warehouses and the backs of stores and hotels, the Ganongs turned the house around. It was a tacit recognition by one of St. Stephen's most prominent business families that the river was no longer the lifeblood of the town. James Porter's clapboard Georgian house acquired Queen Anne features: verandas, a front gable, a corner tower, and a name: Lonicera, after the honeysuckle that the Ganongs, who were enthusiastic gardeners, grew on the property. Gilbert and Marie Ganong had no children and they arranged that on the death of the surviving partner the house be given to the community as a residence for senior citizens. Gilbert Ganong died in 1917 and Maria in 1934.

TODD HOUSE, DOVER HILL, ST. STEPHEN

Until appropriated by Loyalists, flat-topped Dover Hill, overlooking the Schoodic Falls, was a summer campsite for Passamaquoddy Indians. The first permanent house on the site was built in 1808 by Joseph Clarke and occupied by his brother the Reverend Richard Clarke, the first rector of Christ Church, St. Stephen. In 1839, Freeman H. Todd, lumber baron, ship-owner, mill-owner and lumber merchant bought the property, remodelled the house and landscaped the grounds. To the exterior he added sweeping balconies, curved glass windows, verandas and a cupola; to the interior he added high ceilings, hand-carved fireplaces and fine archways. On the death of Freeman Todd in 1885 the house was taken over by his daughter Addie and her husband, Charles W. Young of Calais, a prominent lumber merchant and president of the St. Croix Soap Manufacturing Company. From 1938, when the Todd Family sold it, until 1956, when it was damaged by fire, the house functioned as the Dover Hill Inn. After the fire the building was used as a manufactory for bags, boxes, and textiles and, finally, after yet another conversion, as an office building for the provincial government. The building was demolished in 1996 and the property is now a municipal park.

TODD HALL, UNION STREET, ST. STEPHEN

William F. Todd, the youngest son of Freeman H. Todd, inherited his father's taste for large, colourful houses. The style of his Union Street house is Second Empire, made popular during the reign of Napoleon III of France (1852-1870). No style could be farther from colonial or Georgian restraint and no expense was spared in executing it. Using southern cypress, oak and black walnut, carpenters worked for two years on the interior woodwork alone. Even the fittings in the horse stalls of the carriage house were of brass. Up to four hundred guests could be entertained in the ballroom floor of the main house. William F. Todd was a businessman and a public servant. He represented Charlotte County in both the Provincial Assembly and the House of Commons, and from 1923-1928 he was lieutenant-governor of New Brunswick.

Todd Hall, Union Street, St. Stephen

Governor General Lord Willingdon and Lady Willingdon and Lieutenant Governor and Mrs. Todd. Photographed in front of the Todd House on the occasion of the Governor General's visit to St. Stephen and St. Andrews in July 1927.

CULLINEN HOUSE/ELM HALL, WATER STREET, ST. STEPHEN

In the late 1860s, Hugh Cullinen, a textile magnate from Saint John, built this large Italianate house on a site overlooking Water Street. The house remained a private residence until 1900 when Ganong Brothers bought it for use as a boarding house for young female workers from Newfoundland, Ireland, and Scotland. All were tightly supervised and chaperoned by the warden, Mrs. Wallace Towers. From the 1930s to the 1970s the building served as a hotel, the Park Hotel, and since 1976 it has been the home of St. Stephen University.

MARKS STREET SCHOOL

Designed by architect Matthew Hannah and landscaped by Samuel Almond, Marks Street High School was one of the most elegant public buildings in the St. Croix Valley. Hannah used the villas of Renaissance Italy as models—compact vertical buildings with doorways arranged symmetrically in the façade, and tall, arched or canopied windows. Like many of the villas, the roof was hipped and surmounted by a tall bell tower culminating in an elegant finial. The stone for the foundation and for the trim in the walls was cut and laid by Alfred Price, a master stonecutter from England. The granite for the foundation and the trim came from the Ledge, and the bricks, which were the main building material, likely came from a brickyard in Calais. The approach to the school was a tree-lined gravel walk that swept gracefully around the building. The trees were planted on Arbor Day in May 1885 to honour deserving citizens of the town.

Victory Garden, Marks Street School

Victory Gardens were part of the civilian war effort in both World Wars. To avert the danger of food shortages and direct resources to military ends, communities were encouraged to become as self-sufficent as possible.

Chipman Memorial Hospital

Yet another large St. Stephen house subjected to recycling in the twentieth century was the home of the shipbuilder Zachariah Chipman. Given to the community in memory of Mrs Chipman, the house became a hospital in 1902. For many years it was the largest and best staffed hospital in the region, and several Calais physicians sent their patients there. So many babies of Calais parents were born in the Chipman (70-80 annually) that a Maine public health official became alarmed at the distortion of the town's vital statistics. As a result, it became the practice during the 1930s to register such births at the United States Consulate in St. Stephen. The anomaly prompted Ernest Fitzpatrick, the consul at the time, to write an article, "A Unique Consular District," for *The Foreign Service Journal.*

Calais Free Library

One of the seldom-noted losses in the great 1870 fire was Calais's first public library, a collection of a few thousand books housed in a downtown office building. The library's post-fire home was on the third floor of the Pike Opera building which, partly through donations at first, quickly began to fill with books. Borrowers paid a small quarterly membership fee. This arrangement lasted until the death of James Shepherd Pike in 1882. In his will, Pike left his riverbank town house, formerly the homestead of his father, William Pike, to the community on condition that it be used as a free library and reading room. But the prospect of housing what by then had become a substantial collection of books in a vulnerable frame building alarmed two of the border communities' most prominent citizens, Frederick A. Pike of Calais, James Shepherd's younger brother, and Freeman H. Todd of St. Stephen. Both men donated five thousand dollars toward the cost of a new, fire-resistant building. William Pike's house was moved to Calais Avenue to be replaced, in 1892, by a trim, neo-Gothic building with a turret, a slate roof, and walls of buff brick edged with stone—the Calais Free Library.

Image Sources

Charlotte County Archives: pages 8, 10, 12(upper), 14, 16, 18, 29, 66(lower), 73, 83, 114, 118
Charlotte County Museum: pages 2, 3(lower), 5, 6, 9, 13, 15, 24, 27, 35(upper), 36(upper), 37, 42(upper), 51, 55, 62, 64, 65, 68, 70, 74, 88, 89, 91(lower), 92(upper), 97, 100, 113, 116, 118, 130, 131, 132, 133, 135(upper), 136
Calais Free Library: pages ix, 3(upper),17, 20, 21(upper), 22, 23, 30, 35(lower), 38, 46, 52, 53, 54, 57, 58, 67(lower), 72, 75, 77, 78, 79, 80, 81, 82, 85, 86, 87, 92(lower), 95, 101, 106, 107(upper), 109, 110(upper), 112(upper), 115, 117, 119, 120, 123, 124, 125, 126, 135(lower)
Maine Historic Preservation Commission: pages 127, 128
Moffatt, Tom: page 5
New Brunswick Museum: page 12(lower)
Private Collection: pages 2, 4, 129
Provincial Archives of New Brunswick: pages 1, 7, 11, 21(lower), 26(lower), 28, 40, 41, 42(lower), 43, 44, 45, 56, 59, 60, 66(upper), 67(upper), 69, 71, 76, 84, 98, 99, 107(lower), 111, 112(lower), 121, 122, 134
St. Croix Historical Society: pages 19, 25, 26(upper), 29, 31, 32, 33, 34, 36(lower), 39 47, 48, 49, 50, 61, 75(lower), 90, 91(upper), 93, 94, 96, 102, 108, 110(lower)